D1709018

FRENCH

DESSERTS

Pièce du Boucher

Entrecôte Beurre Maître d'Hôtel 15-

Desserts Maison

tarte aux Pommes   6 -
tarte Nectarine   7 -
crème brûlée   5 -
Mousse Chocolat   5 -
Compote Pommes   5 -
Fauselle au Miel   5 -

Vins de Propriété

FRENCH
DESSERTS

HILLARY DAVIS

photographs by STEVEN ROTHFELD

GIBBS SMITH
TO ENRICH AND INSPIRE HUMANKIND

First Edition
20 19 18 17 16   5 4 3 2 1

Text © 2016 Hillary Davis
Photographs © 2016 Steven Rothfeld

All rights reserved. No part of this book may be reproduced by any means whatsoever without written permission from the publisher, except brief portions quoted for purpose of review.

Published by
Gibbs Smith
P.O. Box 667
Layton, Utah 84041

1.800.835.4993 orders
www.gibbs-smith.com

Designed by Sheryl Dickert
Printed and bound in Hong Kong

Also by Hillary Davis
Le French Oven
French Comfort Food
Cuisine Niçoise: Sun-Kissed Cooking from the French Riviera
A Million a Minute

Gibbs Smith books are printed on either recycled, 100% post-consumer waste, FSC-certified papers or on paper produced from sustainable PEFC-certified forest/controlled wood source. Learn more at www.pefc.org.

Library of Congress Cataloging-in-Publication Data

Names: Davis, Hillary, 1952- author. | Rothfeld, Steven, photographer.
Title: French desserts / Hillary Davis ; photographs by Steven Rothfeld.
Description: First edition. | Layton, Utah : Gibbs Smith, [2016] | Includes index.
Identifiers: LCCN 2016007409 | ISBN 9781423642992 (hardcover)
Subjects: LCSH: Desserts. | Cooking, French. | LCGFT: Cookbooks
Classification: LCC TX773 .D29525 2016 | DDC 641.5944--dc23
LC record available at https://lecn.loc.gov/2016007409

Cuisine de Tradition

CONTENTS

INTRODUCTION

My passion for all things sweet began, as it does for most of us, in my childhood. My grandmother would take us into New York City to a restaurant that made the most incredible mile-high Southern caramel cake. I still dream about it. My father would make us Crêpes Suzette if we asked him. The theatricality of it mesmerized us as he made it right at the table with a burner and copper skillet he bought in France just for the purpose of making the dish. He furthered the evolution of our taste for sweets by arriving home with boxes of baklava from a Greek bakery or with quarts of just-made vanilla ice cream from a local farm.

By age twelve, I was baking creamy rice puddings and making ice creams in our family's old hand-cranked ice cream maker with the sweet peaches

from our trees. By the time I was a newlywed living in Paris, I had developed a recipe box full of handwritten cards of all the desserts I loved to make.

Years later when my husband and I returned to France to make it our home, I gained considerable knowledge about French desserts while living there for almost thirteen years, most of that time next door to a neighbor with a sweet tooth. Madame took me on a culinary tour of France's sweets by tutoring me in her kitchen. She had grown up in Alsace, spent time in Dijon, and moved with her husband to the south of France, so her sweets reflected a wide range of regional specialties.

That sparked my interest in learning more about French cuisine and its deliriously delicious desserts. My husband and I traveled extensively throughout the country, and I was always stopping in local pastry shops to search out and sample things I was unfamiliar with, to explore desserts on bistro menus, and to collect recipes and techniques from people I met as I traveled. My dessert trail was filled with crumbs.

I learned that France has many regional desserts that are not found in other parts of the country, some of which date back centuries. Regional desserts, for the most part, reflect the area they are made in, just as any other dish on the table would. Normandy and Brittany are known for their excellent butter, cream, and milk, so their desserts are butter-centric, while in Provence you are less likely to find a rich, buttery dessert. Regional desserts also evolved because a town or area wanted to promote it for tourism or to protect it as a tradition. Many of the regional desserts I had never seen before in cookbooks, so for that reason, and because I fell in love with them, I made every effort to include them in this, my first dessert cookbook.

You will be delighted with the recipe for a Giant Break-and-Share Cookie (page 69) from the Poitou-Charentes region of France. It is a communal cookie made so that, after town meetings, baptisms, and marriages, everyone can break off a piece to enjoy together. It's my favorite cookie ever. Absolutely delicious. You will also discover a recipe for a unique triangular anise cookie from Charentes, in the western part of central France that is always made on Palm Sunday. Why three-sided? Some say it is to represent the Father, Son, and Holy Ghost. There's a recipe for a sweet sugar bread from the Ardennes region in northern France as well as one for a beautiful ruffled apple pie, called Pastis Gascon (page 196), that they make in southwest France. You'll also love the recipe for little cakes from the area around Dijon, called Nonnettes (page 187), that have an orange marmalade heart.

What I learned over the many years I lived in France and from my extensive traveling throughout the country, is that French desserts—the ones the French make in their homes—are easy to make. Sophisticated pastries are a high art in France and with so many wonderful pastry shops within a short walk, the French simply buy them. They don't make them at home. What they do make at home are the desserts they grew up with—simple, homey comfort food desserts.

With my guidance you will be able to make them in your home kitchen, without fuss or intricate methods or special ingredients. To organize them, I divide each chapter, first into the recipes that are *quicker* to make, followed by the recipes that take

longer to make. And, for the few fancier creations, I worked to demystify the magic of making them. For example, instead of presenting you with a traditional recipe for a *millefeuille,* a complicated and very popular pastry in France, I created one for you to make that is simpler than making cookies and is spectacular when brought to the table.

During a recent interview, a journalist asked me if there was a common theme between the four French cookbooks I have written, and I replied that there is. It is that I wanted to emphasize that French cooking is home cooking. The French go to fancy restaurants if they want fancy food, but for everyday dining, they celebrate simple food made at home, because they treasure their time at the table with family and friends, and they love to cook for them. Cooking and

eating together is a ritual they honor. And the food they honor is the food their grandmother or mother made for them—casual rather than formal, free form rather than fussy.

A word about ingredients. Since the recipes in this book are for the most part based upon only a few ingredients—flour, butter, milk, eggs, and fresh fruit and berries—you should do as the French do and use nothing but the best. Do this, and your desserts will be simply sensational.

I hope you have a great time with these recipes and that they will inspire you and acquaint you with the fabulous regional desserts of France.

Please feel free to email me with your questions or observations at hillarydavis@me.com, I look forward to hearing from you!

ESSENTIAL INGREDIENTS

You can raise the level of your dessert making by living by one simple rule: use nothing but the best ingredients. Other than fresh ingredients, stocking your pantry with essential items like the ones suggested below will give you the flexibility for spontaneous last-minute preparation of desserts without having to go out shopping.

ON THE PANTRY SHELF

ALMOND FLOUR I always have bags of Bob's Red Mill almond flour and hazelnut flour around for making desserts. I love the texture and added flavor they provide compared to using ordinary flour, and they have the added benefit of allowing you to bake gluten free if you wish.

ALMOND PASTE Almond paste is a mixture of almost equal parts of corn syrup or honey, ground almonds, confectioner's sugar, and sometimes almond extract. You can find it in the baking section of most supermarkets. Marzipan, on the other hand, is only ⅓ ground almonds and the rest mostly sugar and is good for forming small candies because it is stiff and a bit dry.

ANISE SEEDS These come from a member of the carrot family and are used to impart a lovely licorice flavor, as does anise extract.

BAKING POWDER This is a leavening agent used in baking. If you run out, make your own by sifting 4 tablespoons baking powder with ½ cup cream of tartar. To test if your baking powder is still good, add 1 teaspoon to 1 cup of hot tap water. If it shows life and foams and bubbles, you are fine to use it. If not, throw it away and buy fresh baking powder.

BAKING SODA This is also a leavening agent, added to baked goods to make them rise.

CAKE FLOUR Use cake flour rather than all-purpose flour when you want a lighter more delicate texture for a cake. It has less gluten than regular flour.

CANDIED FRUIT Use the best you can find online. In a pinch, use candied fruit from the supermarket or a gourmet store near you.

CHOCOLATE Please use semisweet chocolate (unless otherwise indicated) with over 70 percent cocoa solids, as it sets more quickly and has a richer flavor. When using white chocolate in a recipe, make sure that it lists cocoa butter, sugar, and milk as its ingredients—not vegetable fat.

COCOA POWDER I use Hershey's Special Dark Cocoa unsweetened cocoa powder. Unsweetened cocoa powder is one of the most visually appealing garnishes for baked desserts.

CONDENSED MILK Every now and then I come across a recipe that I want to try and it calls for condensed milk, so I usually keep a couple of cans on the shelf. It is made from whole milk that has had some of its moisture removed and has sugar added.

CONFECTIONER'S SUGAR Always have this on hand as so many recipes call for it and because it is a great garnish sifted over a dessert. Powdered sugar and confectioner's sugar are the same.

COOKIES Keeping beautiful high-quality store-bought cookies on the shelf can add a quick, simple flourish to even the simplest dessert. I always stock very thin butter cookies.

CORN SYRUP Dark corn syrup has a deep, strong flavor because molasses has been added, while clear light corn syrup has a lighter flavor. I always keep light corn syrup on hand to use as a gloss for baked pastries and crusts.

CORNSTARCH A must-have thickening agent for various desserts.

HORTENSIA
Hortensi
La plante =
cache pot = 5€
Gardé
La plante =
cache pot = 6

CREAM OF TARTAR Adding a pinch of cream of tartar to room temperature egg whites when you beat them encourages them to reach maximum volume.

DRIED FRUIT Dried fruits have different rehydration methods, so check their packages for instructions.

ESPRESSO POWDER I love using instant espresso powder in desserts for a punch of flavor that often goes unrecognized yet adds a certain something to a combination of flavors. It also means that I can incorporate a coffee flavor without adding more liquid to a recipe. My favorite brand is Medaglia D'Oro, which can be found in most supermarkets and on Amazon.com.

EXTRACTS Keep pure lemon, orange, vanilla, almond, and anise extracts to impart added flavor to your desserts. Always use pure extracts as imitation extracts impart an unpleasant flavor and defeat the purpose of making a wonderful-tasting dessert.

FLOUR All-purpose unbleached flour, bread flour, cake flour, whole-wheat flour, and pastry flour should be kept on hand and always in an airtight container or resealable plastic bag as humidity will deteriorate them. I use King Arthur flours, and if I can't find them, I order them online.

To make your own cake flour, measure out 1 cup of all-purpose flour, remove 2 tablespoons and replace them with 2 tablespoons cornstarch. Always measure flour before sifting.

FLOWERS Edible flowers, preferably from your garden and unsprayed with pesticides, add a whimsical touch to almost any dessert.

FRESHNESS I know. This sounds obvious. But I need to emphasize how important fresh ingredients are, especially when you are using fruit, herbs, eggs, and milk when making desserts. Freshness improves the intensity and quality of flavor and provides the

platform for the dessert to be elevated to something special instead of ordinary. If possible, cook from your garden, pick from your neighbors' trees, shop from local farms and farm stands, and remember to buy local so your ingredients haven't had to be shipped by train or truck.

FRUIT Thoroughly wash and dry fruit before using and, when possible, choose organic and local. In a pinch, buy frozen fruit. It's actually quite good, as it is picked fresh and flash frozen. All you have to do is defrost it.

GELATIN Made from animal collagen, gelatin is used to gel many desserts. If you use gelatin sheets, one sheet equals 1 teaspoon of powdered gelatin.

If you are a vegetarian, you can purchase agar-agar, which is derived from algae, or Vegan Jel, which is made from vegetable gum, and follow the instructions on the package.

GINGER, CRYSTALIZED Purchase crystalized ginger and keep it on the shelf for chopping into desserts or cakes.

HONEY Honey adds moistness and helps extend shelf life in baked goods, plus it adds another layer of

flavor. I like to keep an aromatic flower honey on the shelf as well as a darker honey for a stronger flavor.

JAMS AND PRESERVES I have jars of raspberry, strawberry, orange, and apricot jams on my shelf, as well as cherry preserves, and pick up unusual ones on my travels to inspire me to create new desserts with them.

LIQUEURS AND SPIRITS The French tend to use liqueurs and spirits in their desserts. The top French brands they use are Pastis or Pernod, licorice-flavored liqueurs; Cointreau or Grand Marnier, which are made from oranges; Calvados, which is made from apples; Chartreuse, which is made by Carthusian monks from 130 plants and herbs; Chambord, a liqueur made from raspberries; and Armagnac and Cognac, both brandies.

NUTS Almonds, pistachios, walnuts, pine nuts, and hazelnuts are all popular in French desserts. Nuts kept in a warm place can turn rancid, so when you buy them, store any leftovers in the freezer or refrigerator.

RAISINS AND CURRANTS Although not an essential ingredient, raisins and currants will keep in

an airtight container if kept in a cool, dark place through their entire best-before date on the package, so they can be added to your supplies if you wish.

RICE Almost any kind of rice can be used in making desserts. I generally use short-grain rice or basmati rice in my dessert making.

SALT I prefer to use kosher, sea salt, or fleur de sel in all my recipes, especially because everyday table salt contains chemicals.

SPICES Rather than buying spices in bulk, buy them in small quantities as they can lose their intensity over time. To build your spice rack for making desserts, begin with the following: ground and whole cinnamon, ground and whole nutmeg, ground ginger, ground cardamom, ground and whole cloves, star anise, anise seeds, and fennel seeds.

SUGARS Always have on hand a selection of sugars: granulated, superfine, and confectioner's, as well as light brown for adding a butterscotch flavor to desserts and dark brown, which is granulated sugar to which molasses has been added, to add a deep color and distinctive rich flavor. Keep turbinado, clear, colored, or sparkling sugars to give cookies and crusts a crunchy top.

Store sugars in airtight containers to avoid their absorbing humidity and becoming hardened or lumpy. I keep mine in large glass jars with screw-top lids.

SYRUPS A good selection of bottled syrups in your pantry enhances your ability to improvise when making desserts. Keep a bottle of black currant syrup, orange flower water syrup, or a good quality chocolate syrup on hand to drizzle back and forth over your desserts.

VANILLA BEANS While Tahitian vanilla beans are popular and exude a lovely perfumed flavor, most of the time I prefer Mexican vanilla beans, which impart a stronger flavor.

VANILLA EXTRACT I make my own, using the seeds from 3 to 4 vanilla beans added to 1 cup dark rum, vodka, or bourbon and storing it in the refrigerator for five weeks before using it. For my pantry, I keep the best-quality store-bought pure vanilla extract, such as Mexican vanilla extract, Nielsen Massey Madagascar vanilla extract, Penzeys double-strength vanilla extract, or a good-quality vanilla paste.

YEAST I use active dry yeast, which is available in most supermarkets. You just add warm water and it comes to life. If it does not come to life, or "bloom," throw it out and repeat with a new package. Check the date of shelf life, printed on the packet, before buying.

ZEST Try to use only organic unwaxed citrus fruit to avoid ingesting pesticides and wax, and always thoroughly wash the fruit before working with it. Citrus zest comes from the outside peel of the fruit, culling the flavorful oil from the fruit and making it an essential ingredient when you want to intensify a citrus flavor. I use either a citrus zester, a citrus microplane, or the big holes of a box grater.

IN THE FREEZER OR REFRIGERATOR

BUTTER I use unsalted and salted butters, and I prefer ones wrapped in foil as butter tends to pick up flavors in the refrigerator. No substitutes should be used for butter unless specifically noted in the instructions. To soften butter, take it out of the refrigerator and let it sit for an hour and a half, until it is soft enough to squeeze. I keep a good supply in the freezer and pull it out and thaw as needed.

If you only have salted butter, omit the salt in the recipe. There is approximately ½ teaspoon of salt in 1 stick of salted butter.

BUTTERMILK The French use *lait fermenté,* which is similar to buttermilk. If you don't have butter-milk, make your own by gently warming 1 cup milk.

Add 1 tablespoon lemon juice and let it stand for 15 minutes. Et voila!

CREAM I use heavy whipping cream or heavy cream for desserts, which both have higher butterfat content than whipping cream. When whipping for volume, it is best to chill the beaters as well as the bowl and cream.

EGGS Please use large eggs unless otherwise noted, preferably organic or free range. In baking, whole eggs are essential for leavening, while beating the egg whites separately from the yolks then folding them in will greatly increase the loft and lightness of a baked item. When you beat a yolk or white with a little water then paint it onto an unbaked crust, it creates a beautiful golden-brown baked crust. Make sure to take the eggs out of the refrigerator and let them come to room temperature before using.

In non-baked items, eggs add richness, structure, thickness, color, and flavor.

EGG WHITES If you have leftover egg whites from a recipe, you can put them in a screw-top glass jar or covered container in the refrigerator for up to 1 week or 10 days. Egg whites may also be frozen and used later.

FROZEN FRUIT Having assorted bags of frozen fruit on hand in the freezer gives you immense flexibility in preparing desserts at the last minute or when you don't have access to fresh fruit.

FROZEN PHYLLO DOUGH Phyllo is paper-thin sheets of dough and has a myriad of uses for making desserts. It can also be very effective in creating a stunning visual presentation. Once you thaw it and as you use it, keep it covered so that it does not dry out. It will keep in your freezer for 6 months.

FROZEN PUFF PASTRY I can't imagine living without frozen puff pastry in my freezer. The busy lives we lead today leave us little time to work up

a magnificent homemade puff pastry. I buy mine frozen, as most French households do, and always have it on hand.

HERBS Increasingly I am using fresh herbs and even vegetables when I am creating desserts because I am fascinated with the surprisingly lovely flavors that evolve from them. You will find recipes in this cookbook, for example, using fresh tarragon or basil. I often blend rosemary and honey, sage and lemon juice, mint and simple syrup, fresh lavender and simple syrup, and other variations of herbs and sweeteners to use as sweet sauces or to make sorbets or ice creams. Keep fresh herbs in a glass of water in the refrigerator if you are not using them within a couple of days of purchase.

ICE CREAM AND SORBET Always have at least one fruit sorbet and a basic vanilla ice cream in the freezer, especially in the summer, for improvising a dessert in a bowl. A little drizzle of chocolate sauce and a couple of store-bought cookies and it starts to look pretty interesting.

LEMONS As a lemon lover, I always have a quantity of lemons on hand to use in making desserts and for preventing freshly cut fruit from turning brown or oxidizing. Lemon zest, either from a microplane or box grater, adds a zing of flavor and color to almost any sweet. Make sure to zest only from organic unwaxed lemons.

MILK I use whole milk or almond milk for my recipes.

NUTS Store well-wrapped nuts in the refrigerator for up to 3 months or in the freezer for 6 months. ❧

ESSENTIAL TOOLS

BAKING SHEETS A few baking sheets, at least, should always be on hand. You can never have enough baking sheets.

BLOWTORCH Although not required for any of the recipes in this cookbook, I think every kitchen should have a culinary blow torch. They are perfect for last-minute browning of meringue and for making a brûlée top for custards.

BOX GRATER You probably already have one. These are handy for grating chocolate and zesting citrus rind.

CANDY THERMOMETER To cook sugar for various desserts, you will need a candy thermometer. When you purchase a new one, test to see if it is accurate by dipping it into boiling water to see if it reaches boiling point—212 degrees F. The most important thing to know about using a candy thermometer is to remove it from the cooking mixture 1 or 2 degrees before it reaches the desired temperature, as the mixture will continue to cook when removed from heat. Buy a good-quality thermometer that reaches up to 400 degrees F.

COOKIE SCOOPS Available at most kitchen supply stores, these ensure that each cookie has an exact amount of dough so they all come out the same size.

CUTTERS Keep a supply of cookie cutters and assorted round cutters to cut cake.

CUTTING BOARDS Although I have been given some beautiful wooden cutting boards as gifts, I reserve them for savory cooking and use only plastic cutting boards that will not retain flavors or odors for my dessert making.

DIGITAL TIMER A good digital timer is essential to making many of the desserts in this cookbook for preparation times, cooking, and baking times. Having more than one is helpful.

ELECTRIC BLENDER For quick batters, making crêpes, waffle batter, and sauces, a blender comes in very handy.

ELECTRIC HAND MIXER Instead of whisking by hand, a small electric hand mixer speeds up the process and lessens the amount of work involved in creating volume with ease.

ELECTRIC STAND MIXER I cannot live without my KitchenAid mixer. A heavy-duty stand mixer on a sturdy base with whisk and paddle attachments is one of the must-haves for making many desserts. A trick I learned from my father is to have two or three mixing bowls and whisks for the mixer so you can beat egg yolks, then switch bowls and whisks and beat egg whites, and if asked for, do another switch to beat heavy cream—without having to stop and wash a bowl and whisk to do each procedure. If budget permits, it is a labor-saving solution.

FOOD PROCESSOR My food processor of choice has always been a Cuisinart, and I do everything in it. For desserts, it is indispensable.

ICE CREAM MACHINE I make lots of sorbets and ice creams in the summer. I love fresh fruit sorbets and using unusual ingredients to make ice creams. If you make frozen treats often, purchase the best ice cream machine within your budget, as it will last longer and work more efficiently and quickly.

ICE CREAM SCOOP Get a couple of sizes of scoops, small and large, round or oval, to scoop your home-made ice creams and sorbets. Also have one with a sweeping blade for scooping batters and doughs.

INSTANT-READ THERMOMETER For testing the temperature of liquid before dissolving active dry yeast, it is easiest to use an instant-read thermometer. It is also very helpful in making candies.

KNIVES Sharp knives of all sizes and a good sharpener are needed, as well as a palette knife for frosting cakes.

MEASURING CUPS One or two sets of measuring cups, from $1/8$ cup to 1 cup, are a must for measuring dry ingredients. Clear glass measuring cups for liquids, including 1-cup, 2-cup, and 4-cup sizes, are important to have so you can use more than one during a recipe without having to stop and wash it.

MEASURING SPOONS One or two sets of measuring spoons, from $1/8$ teaspoon to 1 table-spoon, are valuable to have when baking.

MEASURING TAPE I keep a measuring tape in my pastry equipment drawer as I often want to measure a rolled-out pastry so that I can cut it into squares or triangles or to fit it into a specific baking pan.

MICROPLANE You will need a citrus microplane and, perhaps, one with larger holes if you would like to grate chocolate.

MINI MUFFIN TINS These are useful for making bite-size treats as well as tiny muffins.

MIXING BOWLS At the minimum you should have a small, medium, and large set of mixing bowls, as well as a medium-size heatproof bowl.

NUTMEG GRINDER Spices taste much better if they are freshly ground before using, so a nutmeg grater dedicated to grinding a whole nutmeg is a must.

OVEN THERMOMETER Every time I use a different oven in a different location or house or even professional kitchen, I always check it first with an oven thermometer because all ovens vary due to age, how heavily they have been used, and how well they have been maintained. If oven temperatures are not accurate, then baking times will not be accurate and recipes will not work as they should. In addition to the condition of each and every oven, baking at different altitudes will alter results. In fact, I use an oven thermometer every time I bake, just to make sure.

Follow the timing directions for the recipes in this cookbook, but always begin to visually check about 10 minutes before and then every 5 minutes thereafter to assure that your baked dessert looks good and a tester comes out clean. Especially when you are baking desserts, attaining and maintaining the correct oven temperature makes the difference between failure and success.

Reduce recommended cooking temperature by 25–50 degrees if you are using a convection oven.

PANS AND MOLDS Recipes in this cookbook will call for removable-bottom tart pans (9-inch and 10-inch, both round and rectangular), springform cake pans (9-inch and 10-inch), round cake pans (8-inch, 9-inch, and at least 2 inches deep), pie dishes, gratin and baking dishes, 8-inch square baking pans, Bundt pans, 8-inch and 9-inch soufflé dishes, and a couple of 9 x 5-inch loaf pans.

PARCHMENT PAPER Buy parchment paper for lining baking sheets and pans to prevent sticking during baking.

PASTRY BRUSHES Any size natural-bristle pastry brush will do. I have a flat one, a large one that looks like a paint brush that I use for dusting flour across dough I want to roll out, and an oval one. I use them for brushing egg washes on tart crusts, for bathing cake layers with syrups, and the oval one I use most for delicate touches of glaze on a thin crust or for dipping into melted chocolate to paint a dessert plate.

PIE WEIGHTS Do you know how much rice and dried beans I have used over the years for weighing down pie and tart crusts? Why didn't I get pie weights sooner? They are great.

ROLLING PINS I have a really heavy old rolling pin I inherited from my grandmother, and I find that the heavier the rolling pin, the easier it is to roll out dough. Find a marble one if you can, and put it in the refrigerator to chill before rolling out your dough. I also have a fun one carved with fleurs-de-lys to roll over pie crust to decorate it. Smaller ones without handles are good for rolling small pastries and flattening cookies.

SPATULAS Have on hand at least two medium-size and two large-size spatulas for using together to lift cakes or breads or to use singly to lift cookies and candies. Have several sizes of flexible rubber spatulas to fold mixtures together.

SPOONS Keep a set of wooden spoons, from small to medium to large, for stirring mixtures on the stove.

STRAINER You should have a fine-mesh wire strainer to sift flours and other dry ingredients.

WHISKS Try to find a hand whisk with a non-slip grip to use for whisking sauces, eggs, and batters.

HOMEY CAKES

C akes made by families in France are simple and look homemade. They are often a single layer, sometimes glazed, served with fruit, and/or whipped cream.

The *quicker* cakes in this chapter are *cakes sucrés*, cakes baked in a loaf pan. Although they are available in supermarkets, most French families make their own and slice them for picnics or for Sunday visits with friends. That's why they are sometimes also referred to as weekend cakes.

The cakes in this chapter that take a bit *longer* to make include a stunning rice pudding cake, a one-layer hazelnut cake from the Creuse region in the very middle of France, an apple cake Tatin style from Normandy, a one-layer light-as-air walnut cake from the Périgord region, and a fabulous butter cake from Brittany.

PLENTY OF PEARS SALTED CARAMEL LOAF CAKE

Gâteau Invisible aux Poires et Caramel au Beurre Salé **QUICKER** | SERVES 8

This is what the French call an invisible cake because so little batter is used to hold together the fruit that you see very little of the cake when it is baked. When you slice it, you see layers and layers of pears, and when you taste it, you have the soft pears playing against a salted-caramel flavor that is achieved by poking holes in the top of the cake and pouring salted caramel over the top so that it seeps in.

SPECIAL EQUIPMENT 1 (9 X 5-INCH) LOAF PAN; PARCHMENT PAPER; ELECTRIC STAND MIXER

Cake

3 large eggs, room temperature

¼ cup sugar

2 teaspoons pure vanilla extract

1 cup all-purpose flour

¼ teaspoon salt

¼ cup unsalted butter, melted

½ cup half-and-half

2 pounds (3 to 4) firm pears

Topping and Sauce

½ cup light brown sugar

½ cup half-and-half

4 tablespoons salted butter

½ teaspoon salt

CAKE

Preheat oven to 400 degrees F. Line the loaf pan with parchment paper cut so that it overhangs the short sides by 2 inches and another piece of parchment paper cut so that it overhangs the long sides by 2 inches. You will use these overhangs as a sling to lift the cake out of the pan after it is baked.

Using the mixer, beat the eggs with the sugar until pale and thick, about 3 minutes. Add the vanilla and beat to combine. Add the flour, salt, butter, and half-and-half; mix until combined.

Do not peel the pears. Simply cut them into very thin slices and stir them into the batter. It will look like it is all pears, and you will not see much batter once it is all mixed.

Scoop this mixture into the loaf pan, pat it down flat, and bake for 45–55 minutes, until a tester comes out clean. Take the cake out of the oven, and increase the oven temperature to 425 degrees F.

TOPPING AND SAUCE

Heat the brown sugar, half-and-half, butter, and salt in a saucepan until it comes to a boil then let it bubble away for 2 minutes.

Poke holes in the top of the cake with a fork or a skewer. Pour half of the hot caramel mixture over the cake and place the cake back into the oven to bake for another 12 minutes. Reserve the remaining sauce.

Remove the cake from the oven, cool for 5 minutes, then gently lift with the parchment paper and slip the cake onto a serving plate. Remove the parchment paper and cool to room temperature for 20 minutes.

To serve, use a serrated knife to gently cut the cake into 1-inch-thick slices and ladle a bit of warm caramel sauce over the top.

WHOLE WHEAT NUTELLA LOAF CAKE

Cake Complet au Nutella **QUICKER** | SERVES 8

One day I was watching my friend spread Nutella on a slice of loaf cake for her son's afternoon snack, and I thought how nice it would be if the Nutella was baked into the cake as well and served warm. I developed this recipe with that vision in mind. The alluring combination of chocolate- hazelnut swirls of Nutella and the sweet cake only gets better a day later.

SPECIAL EQUIPMENT 1 (9 X 5-INCH) LOAF PAN

1 ¾ cups whole-wheat flour

2 ½ teaspoons baking powder

¼ teaspoon salt

½ cup vegetable oil

¾ cup granulated sugar

¼ cup light brown sugar

1 ½ teaspoons pure vanilla extract

½ cup half-and-half

½ cup plain Greek yogurt

3 large eggs, room temperature

⅓ cup plus 2 tablespoons Nutella

Preheat oven to 350 degrees F. Butter and flour the loaf pan.

In a medium mixing bowl, add the flour, baking powder, and salt and whisk to combine.

In a large mixing bowl, add the oil, granulated sugar, brown sugar, vanilla, half-and-half, and yogurt and whisk well to combine. With a fork, beat the eggs then add them to the bowl, and whisk to combine.

Pour the dry ingredients into the wet ingredients and stir until just combined.

Heat the Nutella in a small saucepan until just melted.

Scoop half of the batter into the loaf pan, spoon on half the Nutella and use a fork to swirl it down into the batter in large curves. Scoop the rest of the batter over the top, spoon on the rest of the Nutella, and use the fork to swirl it into the batter.

Bake for 55 minutes, or until a skewer comes out clean. Cool the cake for 5 minutes in the pan then transfer to a serving plate.

TART LIME AND YOGURT LOAF CAKE

Gâteau au Yaourt et au Citron Vert QUICKER | SERVES 8

There are recipes I found in cooking magazines in France where you make a yogurt cake using the yogurt containers to measure the ingredients! One I remember trying tasted delicious made with banana yogurt and sliced bananas. After a while I developed this recipe, and now it is my favorite rendition because I love the combination of tart limes and the tangy yogurt in a sweet cake. I dress it up with a sweet lime glaze and candied lime slices.

SPECIAL EQUIPMENT 1 (9 X 5-INCH) LOAF PAN; FOOD PROCESSOR; CITRUS MICROPLANE

Cake

1 ½ cups granulated sugar

3 organic limes

2 cups all-purpose flour

2 ½ teaspoons baking powder

¼ teaspoon salt

2 large eggs

1 large egg yolk

4 tablespoons vegetable oil

1 tablespoon unsalted butter, melted

1 cup plain Greek or regular yogurt

1 teaspoon pure vanilla extract

Glaze

1 organic lime, juiced

½ cup confectioner's sugar

Candied limes

1 organic lime

½ cup water

½ cup granulated sugar

CAKE

Preheat the oven to 350 degrees F. Butter and flour the loaf pan.

Place the sugar into the food processor. Using the microplane, finely grate the zest of 1 lime over the sugar, process for 10 seconds, and then let rest for 10 minutes so the lime oil flavors and scents the sugar.

Squeeze all 3 limes for juice. This should yield approximately ⅓ cup juice. Use all of the juice when asked for it.

Sift the flour, baking powder, and salt into the food processor and pulse 6 times. Transfer this mixture into a mixing bowl.

Place the eggs, egg yolk, oil, butter, yogurt, vanilla, and all the lime juice into the food processor and process for 5 seconds. Add back in the dry ingredients and pulse just until combined, about 4 long pulses.

Pour the batter into the loaf pan and bake for 50–55 minutes, until golden and a tester comes out clean. Remove from the oven, allow to cool for 10 minutes, remove from the pan, wrap completely in plastic wrap to retain moisture, and allow the cake to completely cool.

continued >

GLAZE

Mix the lime juice with the confectioner's sugar. If it needs to be thinner, add a bit of warm water. Remove the plastic wrap from the cake. Pour the glaze all over the cake, attempting to also coat the sides.

CANDIED LIMES

Cut the lime into rounds, as thinly as possible, and remove the pips. Slice the rounds in half to make half moons.

Add the water and sugar to a saucepan, bring to a boil, then reduce to a simmer. Add the lime slices and cook for 5–10 minutes, until the peel is very tender. Leave to cool in the saucepan.

To serve, lay the half-moon slices of lime down one side of the cake, with the cut side facing outwards along one edge, then present the whole cake on a serving tray or plate.

TIP

This recipe also makes 12 muffins. Try it using lime-flavored yogurt for an additional punch of lime flavor.

WINE AND GRAPE HARVEST LOAF CAKE

Cake au Vin Blanc des Vendanges QUICKER | SERVES 8

"It is celestial food to eat for breakfast hot fresh cake with grapes . . ."—François Rabelais

Warming this cake in the oven then slicing it for breakfast releases a scent of cardamom that is intoxicating. I agree with Rabelais. There's something very special about hot cake with grapes for breakfast, an unusual pairing but absolutely celestial.

I also make this when I have wine and cheese parties and serve it sliced next to a bowl of grapes and wedges of cheese. The grapes inside of the cake complement salty cheese really well.

SPECIAL EQUIPMENT 1 (9 X 5-INCH) INCH LOAF PAN; PARCHMENT PAPER

Cake

2 ¼ cups all-purpose flour

2 ½ teaspoons baking powder

½ teaspoon salt

1 teaspoon ground cardamom

3 large eggs, room temperature, beaten

1 cup plus 3 tablespoons granulated sugar

1 cup plus ¼ cup sweet white wine (Beaume-de-Venise, Riesling, Sauternes, or Moscato), divided

¾ cup vegetable oil

1 ½ teaspoons pure vanilla extract

1 tablespoon organic lemon zest

1 cup red seedless grapes, sliced in half

Glaze

1 cup confectioner's sugar

2 tablespoons sweet white wine

½ teaspoon pure vanilla extract

½ teaspoon ground cardamom

CAKE

Preheat the oven to 350 degrees F. Lightly butter the loaf pan then line the width of the pan with parchment paper, leaving a 2-inch overhang on both sides to use as a sling to help lift the cake out once it is baked.

Sift the flour, baking powder, salt, and cardamom into a medium mixing bowl. Whisk to combine.

In a large mixing bowl, whisk the eggs, sugar, 1 cup wine, oil, vanilla, and lemon zest together. Add the dry ingredients into the bowl and whisk together until blended. Fold in the grapes.

Pour the batter into the loaf pan only until it reaches the rim and discard any excess batter. Bake for 50–55 minutes, until golden and a tester comes out clean. Take out of the oven and leave the cake in the pan.

Heat the remaining wine until it begins to simmer then pour it over the cake. Allow the cake to cool for 10 minutes then remove from pan and place on a wire rack over a sheet of parchment paper.

GLAZE

When the cake has completely cooled, whisk together the confectioner's sugar, wine, vanilla, and cardamom until well blended. Drizzle over the cake. Let the glaze set before slicing the cake.

TIP

To garnish, slice more red grapes and decorate the top of the cake so that every slice gets some of the grapes.

ZUCCHINI, LEMON, AND WALNUT LOAF CAKE

Cake aux Courgettes, au Citron et aux Noix QUICKER | SERVES 8

This cake, bursting with lemony flavor and flecks of green from the zucchini, is so good with tea in the afternoon that it has become a tradition in my house when I have weekend guests. If there's any left over, I serve it for breakfast with a smear of lemon curd.

SPECIAL EQUIPMENT 1 (9 X 5-INCH) LOAF PAN

1 ½ cups all-purpose flour

1 teaspoon baking powder

¼ teaspoon baking soda

¼ teaspoon salt

1 ½ cups coarsely grated zucchini, squeezed very dry in paper towels

1 cup chopped walnuts

1 cup granulated sugar

½ cup olive oil

3 large eggs

½ teaspoon pure vanilla extract

2 teaspoons lemon extract

1 lemon, zested and juiced for ¼ cup juice

Confectioner's sugar

Preheat oven to 325 degrees F. Butter and flour the loaf pan.

In a large mixing bowl, sift together the flour, baking powder, baking soda, and salt. Add the zucchini and walnuts and stir to coat.

In another bowl, whisk together the sugar, olive oil, eggs, vanilla, lemon extract, lemon juice, and lemon zest.

Stir the dry ingredients into the wet ingredients just until combined. Do not overwork the batter.

Scoop batter into the loaf pan and bake for 1 hour. Remove from the oven and cool in the pan for 15 minutes before turning out onto a serving plate. Lightly dust with confectioner's sugar.

ORANGE-GLAZED APRICOT ALMOND LOAF CAKE

Cake à l'Abricot et aux Amandes Glacé à l'Orange **QUICKER** | SERVES 8

With a light delicate texture, studded with tangy bits of apricot and scented with almond, a slice of this loaf cake serves as a superb stage for a mound of fresh berries topped with whipped cream—softly whipped cream with a dash of almond extract to bring out the almond flavor of the cake.

SPECIAL EQUIPMENT 1 (9 X 5-INCH) LOAF PAN; ELECTRIC STAND MIXER

Cake

2 cups all-purpose flour

1 teaspoon baking powder

¼ teaspoon baking soda

¼ teaspoon salt

1 ½ cups coarsely chopped dried apricots

2 sticks unsalted butter, softened

1 ½ cups plus 2 tablespoons granulated sugar

4 large eggs, room temperature

½ teaspoon pure vanilla extract

2 teaspoons almond extract

1 cup milk

Glaze

1 large organic orange, juiced

1 cup confectioner's sugar

CAKE

Preheat oven to 325 degrees F. Butter and flour the loaf pan.

Sift the flour, baking powder, baking soda and salt together into a bowl and whisk well to combine. Toss in the apricots and stir well to coat.

Using the stand mixer, cream the butter until it is very fluffy and light, scraping down the sides of the bowl a few times, for about 5 minutes. Gradually add the sugar and beat on medium speed for another 7 minutes. Add the eggs, one at a time, beating after each one just until the yolk disappears. Beat in the vanilla and almond extracts.

Add some of the flour mixture to the egg mixture and, with a wooden spoon or rubber spatula, stir it to lightly combine. Alternate adding the flour and the milk and mix just until combined into a batter. Don't overmix.

Transfer the batter to the loaf pan and bake for 1 hour, or until a tester comes out clean.

Take the cake out of the oven and allow it to cool in the pan for 10 minutes. Remove from the pan, wrap completely in plastic wrap to retain moisture, and cool the cake completely.

GLAZE

Preheat oven to 215 degrees F.

Add the orange juice to the confectioner's sugar, bit by bit, until it reaches the desired consistency to easily spread. If it needs thinned, add a small amount of warm water. Make it liquid enough to brush on the top and sides of the cake.

Remove the plastic wrap from the cake. Pour the glaze all over the cake and spread with a pastry brush, coating the top and sides. Place on a baking sheet and put in the oven for 8–9 minutes to dry and harden the icing. Remove from the oven and cool to room temperature before slicing.

CRAZY CHOCOLATE LOAF CAKE WITH FLEUR DE SEL AND ICE CREAM

Cake au Chocolat, Fleur de Sel et Crème Glacée **QUICKER** | SERVES 8

My world stops if I smell chocolate cake baking. Everything becomes slow motion until I can have a slice. So I set out to develop a recipe for a rich deep-chocolate loaf cake that was good enough on its own not to need frosting. I think I've done it.
To crazy it up, I break it in half with my hands while it is still warm from the oven, spoon ice cream into the crevice, and give it a final sifting of cocoa over the top and a sprinkle of crunchy fleur de sel. It's crazy delicious.

SPECIAL EQUIPMENT 1 (9 X 5-INCH) LOAF PAN; ELECTRIC STAND MIXER; 1 BAKING SHEET

7 tablespoons unsalted butter, softened

½ cup granulated sugar

¾ cup light brown sugar

2 large eggs, room temperature

1 tablespoon olive oil

¾ cup milk

¼ cup plain Greek yogurt

3 teaspoons instant espresso powder

1 tablespoon pure vanilla extract

1 ½ cups all-purpose flour

½ teaspoon baking powder

¼ teaspoon baking soda

¼ teaspoon salt

¼ cup plus 3 tablespoons Hershey's Special Dark Cocoa

Coffee ice cream

Cocoa powder

Fleur de sel

Preheat oven to 325 degrees F. Butter and flour the loaf pan.

Using the stand mixer, cream the butter and granulated sugar until light and fluffy, about 3 minutes. Add in the brown sugar and beat until combined.

With a fork, beat the eggs with the oil, add to the butter and sugar mixture, and beat to combine. With a fork, whip the milk, yogurt, espresso and vanilla together; add to the bowl and beat to combine.

Sift the flour, baking powder, baking soda, salt, and cocoa together; add to the bowl and beat until just combined.

Scoop the batter into the loaf pan, place on the baking sheet, and bake for 50–55 minutes, until a tester comes out clean.

Let the cake rest in the pan for 10 minutes then unmold it onto a plate. To serve, break it in half vertically with your hands, scoop some ice cream into the center, sift cocoa over the top, and sprinkle with fleur de sel.

HÉLÈNE'S GRANDMOTHER'S RICE PUDDING CAKE BATHED IN CARAMEL

La Gâteau de Riz au Caramel de la Grand-mère d'Hélène LONGER | SERVES 8

My friend and cookbook author, Hélène Lautier, who lives in Cannes, shared with me her grandmother's technique for making a Gâteau de Riz au Caramel without having to bake it. This is her recipe with a few of my personal touches. I really like this method. It's all done on the stovetop, so I can do other things in the kitchen and only need to stir it occasionally as it cooks. Then I scoop it into a mold, refrigerate it overnight, and it is ready for the next day's dinner.

Gâteau de Riz au Caramel is usually served slightly chilled and cut into slices with a drizzle of the caramel sauce it baked in.

SPECIAL EQUIPMENT ELECTRIC HAND MIXER; 6-CUP SOUFFLÉ DISH

Rice Pudding

2 cups water

¾ cup short-grain or Arborio rice*

4 cups whole milk

½ cup confectioner's sugar

2 tablespoons unsalted butter

2 large eggs

1 large egg yolk

½ cup granulated sugar

3 tablespoons plus 2 teaspoons pure vanilla extract

2 teaspoons ground cardamom

Caramel Syrup

1 cup granulated sugar

RICE PUDDING

Bring the water to a boil in a saucepan, toss in the rice, stir, bring back to a lively simmer, and cook for 4 minutes. Drain the rice and discard the water.

Bring the milk to a boil in a saucepan, watching it carefully as it will rise quickly as it comes to a boil. When it starts to rise, turn off the heat and pour in the confectioner's sugar, rice, and butter. Turn the heat back on, reduce to a simmer, and cook for 25–35 minutes, until all of the milk has been absorbed. It's important to stir frequently, especially at the end, so the rice does not stick to the bottom of the pan and so that it becomes creamy. You will hear a plopping noise towards the end.

With the hand mixer, beat the eggs, egg yolk, granulated sugar, vanilla, and cardamom together until pale and thick. Add to the rice pudding on the stove and stir constantly to blend until it comes to a simmer. Stir while cooking for 1 minute then take off the heat.

CARAMEL SYRUP

Heat the sugar in another saucepan over medium heat without stirring, until it turns liquid and golden brown. You can swirl the pan toward the end to help it along. The darker the color and the longer you cook it, the stronger the taste. Just make sure not to cook it so dark that it becomes bitter. If you go too far, it is simple to start over with another cup of sugar.

Take the caramel syrup off the heat and, being careful not to splash the hot syrup on your skin, pour it into the soufflé dish. Pick up the dish and carefully tilt it to cover the bottom and sides with the syrup. Swirl a second time to give another coat to the sides. Allow to cool to room temperature.

Pour the rice mixture into the caramelized dish. Cool to room temperature, then cover with plastic wrap, and refrigerate overnight.

To serve, place a plate over the top of the dish holding the rice pudding cake and invert it to unmold the cake. Allow any caramel syrup left in the baking dish to drip over the cake.

*Do not rinse the rice as you want its surface starch to help thicken the pudding.

HAZELNUT CAKE WITH NUTELLA DRIZZLE

Gâteau Creusois **LONGER** | SERVES 8

This is a simple hazelnut cake from the Creuse region in the very middle of France, where hazel trees flourish and drop loads of hazelnuts. I added a layer of hazelnut meringue to the top before baking to give it a slight crunch, I crown it with a rustic pastry rope in the shape of a heart, then I drizzle it with warm Nutella because hazelnuts are one of the main ingredients in Nutella. It's a hazelnut cake to the third degree.

SPECIAL EQUIPMENT 1 (8-INCH) ROUND CAKE PAN OR SPRINGFORM PAN; FOOD PROCESSOR; ELECTRIC HAND OR STAND MIXER; 1 BAKING SHEET

Cake

1 cup whole hazelnuts, plus more for garnish

1 cup all-purpose flour

½ teaspoon baking powder

¼ teaspoon salt

1 cup confectioner's sugar

¼ cup light brown sugar

1 stick butter, melted then cooled to room temperature

1 ½ teaspoons vanilla extract or hazelnut extract

5 large egg whites, room temperature

Meringue

1 cup whole hazelnuts

4 large egg whites, room temperature

⅓ cup plus 2 tablespoons granulated sugar

Pastry Rope

1 package ready-made pie pastry

Topping

½ cup Nutella

CAKE

Preheat oven to 350 degrees F. Butter and flour the cake pan.

Add 1 cup hazelnuts to the food processor and process until ground. Transfer them to a large mixing bowl.

Sift the flour, baking powder, and salt into the bowl. Add the confectioner's sugar and brown sugar and whisk well to combine. Add the butter and vanilla and whisk well to combine.

Using the mixer, beat the egg whites until stiff. Add 1/4 of the egg whites into the flour mixture and use a rubber spatula to stir them together to loosen up the flour mixture. Add another 1/4 of the egg whites and stir to combine. Now add the rest of the egg whites, stir, and fold, trying to keep as much volume as possible, until you have just combined everything into a batter. Pour into the cake pan and smooth over the top with the spatula.

MERINGUE

Finely grind the hazelnuts in the food processor. Using the mixer, beat the egg whites until soft peaks form. Add the sugar and beat again until the mixture just begins to stiffen. Gently fold in the ground hazelnuts and spread the meringue over the cake

batter in the baking pan, swirling in the middle to make an attractive pattern. Bake for 30–35 minutes, until a tester comes out clean.

PASTRY ROPE

Cut and roll out the ready-made pastry to a rectangle about 12 inches long. Slice into 6 even strips. Take 3 of them and make a braid. Repeat with the remaining 3 strips.

Line a baking sheet with parchment paper. Lay the braids on the baking sheet and bring them together at the bottom and top to make a heart shape, pinching the dough together to join them. Chill while you preheat the oven to 400 degrees F.

Bake the heart-shaped pastry for 10 minutes, or until a beautiful golden brown. Remove and, when cool enough to touch, gently transfer to the top of the cake. Garnish the cake with some whole hazelnuts.

TOPPING

Melt the Nutella in the microwave, drizzle over the top of the cake, and serve.

TIPS

Since Frangelico is flavored with hazelnuts, try whisking some into the melted Nutella. To make a more festive cake, frost just the top of the cake with Nutella, thoroughly cover with an army of whole hazelnuts, and top with the pastry heart.

NORMANDY APPLE CAKE TATIN STYLE

Gâteau Normand aux Pommes comme une Tatin **LONGER** | SERVES 8

Along the idea of a tarte Tatin, the famous apple tart from Normandy, my rendition produces one that is more like a cake and is moist from the caramel sauce baking down into it. If it's for children, sprinkle with a little confectioner's sugar and serve warm with a scoop of vanilla ice cream or whipped cream. If you are serving it to adults, you can flambé it with Calvados or apple brandy before sprinkling with confectioner's sugar. Add a tablespoon or more of Calvados when you make the whipped cream.

SPECIAL EQUIPMENT 1 (9-INCH) GLASS PIE PLATE; ELECTRIC STAND MIXER; 1 BAKING SHEET

2 Granny Smith apples

½ lemon, juiced

1 ¼ cups plus 3 tablespoons granulated sugar, divided

1 tablespoon water

2 tablespoons plus 1 ½ sticks salted butter, softened

2 cups all-purpose flour

1 ¾ teaspoons baking powder

3 large eggs, room temperature

1 ¼ teaspoons pure vanilla extract

3 tablespoons fresh apple cider or milk

Confectioner's sugar

Peel, core, and cut the apples into eighths. Toss into a bowl of water mixed with the lemon juice.

Pour 1 cup sugar and 1 tablespoon water into a wide-bottom skillet or saucepan. Place over medium-low heat and leave to cook, swirling a couple of times towards the end, until the sugar liquefies. At that point, stir until clear. Watch the sugar cook, and when it just begins to turn an amber caramel color, remove it from the heat. You don't want it to turn a dark color. Add 2 tablespoons butter, whisk to combine, then pour this mixture into the glass pie plate to cover the bottom.

Dry off the apple slices with paper towels and, without touching the hot caramel with your hands, arrange the apple slices over the caramel in a daisy-like pattern.

Preheat the oven to 325 degrees F.

Sift together the flour and baking powder into a mixing bowl.

Using the stand mixer, beat the remaining butter and sugar until it begins to look fluffy. Add the eggs and vanilla and beat to combine. Pour the dry ingredients into the egg mixture alternatively with the cider until a soft batter forms.

Spoon the batter over the apples. Run your hands under water then use your fingers to smooth over the surface of the batter, bringing it right to the edges of the pie plate.

Place the pie plate on the baking sheet and bake for 55–60 minutes, until a tester in the center comes out clean.

Take the cake out of the oven and immediately run a small sharp knife along the outside edges of the cake. Then put on oven mitts to protect your hands from any wayward hot sugar syrup, place a serving plate over the cake, and invert, flipping the cake upside down onto the plate, banging on the counter a couple of times to make sure the cake and apples drop to the plate. If you wait, the caramel will harden and you will not be able to remove the cake from the pie plate.

Remove the pie plate and let the cake stand for 10 minutes. The caramel will have cooked up the sides of the cake, and allowing it to stand will let the sides develop a thin sugar crust. Lightly dust it with confectioner's sugar.

Bring the cake to the table and serve warm with vanilla ice cream or whipped cream. If you bring it to the table on individual dessert plates, sift a little confectioner's sugar on the plates to their edges before placing a slice in the middle for a decorative touch.

WALNUT CAKE WITH WARM HONEY GLAZE

Gâteau aux Noix Glacé au Miel Tiède **LONGER** | SERVES 8

There's no flour in this cake. Its structure comes from 2 cups of walnuts whizzed in a food processor until finely ground. It's airy and light and gluten free, with full-bodied flavor from the walnuts. Glazed with warm honey and topped with more walnuts, it's a comforting treat served with a soft mound of whipped cream.

SPECIAL EQUIPMENT 1 (9-INCH) SQUARE BAKING PAN OR SPRINGFORM PAN; 1 BAKING SHEET; FOOD PROCESSOR; ELECTRIC STAND MIXER

Cake

2 cups whole or chopped walnuts, plus 25 whole ones for garnish

2 teaspoons baking powder

¼ teaspoon salt

7 large eggs, room temperature, separated

1 cup granulated sugar

1 teaspoon pure vanilla extract

1 stick unsalted butter, softened

¼ cup honey

Whipped Cream

1 cup heavy whipping cream

3 tablespoons granulated sugar

1 teaspoon pure vanilla extract

CAKE

Preheat oven to 350 degrees F. Butter and sugar the baking pan and place it on the baking sheet.

Using the food processor, add 2 cups walnuts, baking powder, and salt and process until the walnuts are very finely ground, about 10 seconds.

In the stand mixer, beat the egg yolks with the sugar for 5 minutes, until pale and thick. Add the vanilla and butter and beat to combine. Gently fold the ground walnuts into this mixture, trying to preserve volume.

Beat the egg whites until stiff and gently fold ⅓ into the egg yolk mixture until combined then fold in the remaining egg whites, trying to maintain volume.

Scoop the batter into the baking pan and bake for 30–35 minutes, until a tester comes out clean. Remove from the oven and leave in the pan.

Heat the honey until it liquefies then brush it all over the top of the cake, drizzling any remaining over the center of the cake, and allow the cake to cool in the pan before removing to a serving dish.

WHIPPED CREAM

Whip the cream until soft peaks form, then whip in the sugar and vanilla, and whip again to regain soft peaks. Refrigerate until ready to use.

To serve, make an attractive pattern over the top of the cake with whole walnuts or break them into pieces and scatter across the top. Slice and serve with a dollop of whipped cream on the side.

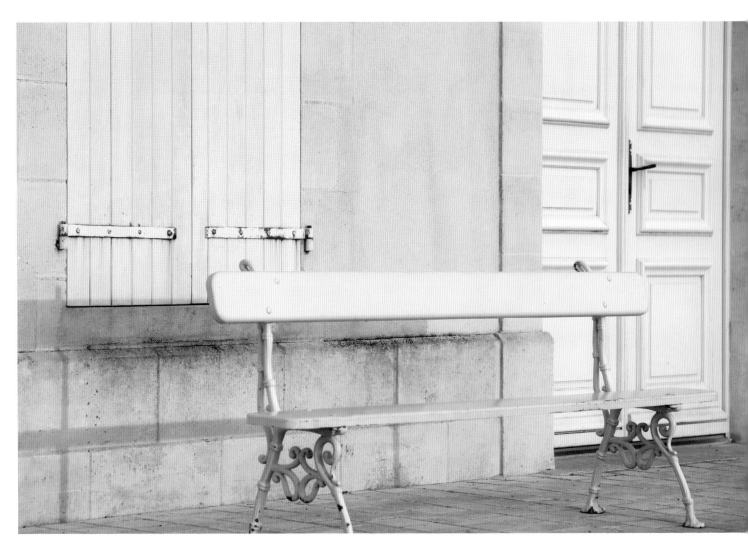

FABULOUS BUTTER CAKE FROM BRITTANY

Le Fabuleux Gâteau Breton LONGER | SERVES 10 TO 12

Brittany sweets are all about the butter, and their famous Gâteau Breton is known for it. Baked in a single layer, it is a dense, decadent, rich butter cake that tastes like shortbread but has the texture of a cake—it is best served in small slices.

It's always made with salted butter, so I also add in a bit of light brown sugar to my version to play up a salted caramel flavor, and I lacquer it towards the end so that it has a slightly shiny exterior. I like baking it just before guests arrive because it fills my kitchen with an aroma that is insane.

SPECIAL EQUIPMENT ELECTRIC STAND MIXER WITH WHISK ATTACHMENT; 1 (9-INCH) SPRINGFORM PAN

Cake

3 sticks salted butter, softened

1 cup granulated sugar

½ cup tightly packed light brown sugar

6 large egg yolks

2 teaspoons pure vanilla extract

2 ⅔ cups all-purpose flour

1 teaspoon baking powder

1 egg beaten with 1 teaspoon water

Lacquer

1 egg beaten with ½ teaspoon water

1 tablespoon light corn syrup

¼ teaspoon pure vanilla extract

CAKE

Generously butter and sugar the springform pan.

Slice the butter into the bowl of the stand mixer. Add the sugars and beat until the mixture is very light and fluffy, about 3 minutes. Add egg yolks and vanilla and mix until well blended.

Sift the flour and baking powder into the bowl and beat on low until just blended. Remove the bowl, scrape down the sides, mix once quickly with a spoon, and then scrape everything into the pan. The dough will be sticky.

Spread the dough into the pan, smoothing the top with the back of a wet spoon or your fingers. Pour half of the egg wash onto the dough and use your fingers to smooth out the top. Pour out any excess egg wash from the cake and discard any remaining wash.

Using a wet fork, press in gently and drag the fork across the surface to make a cross then add in additional fork strokes across the surface in a decorative pattern. Place in the refrigerator for 45 minutes.

After 30 minutes, begin preheating the oven to 325 degrees F.

Aftet the dough has chilled for 45 minutes, bake it in the oven for 45 minutes. Do not remove it from the oven or turn off the heat as the cake will be going back in.

LACQUER

With a fork, beat together the ingredients for the lacquer. Brush the top of the cake with this mixture (it might deflate a little so work quickly) then continue to bake for another 10 minutes, until it has a slightly shiny top and a tester comes out clean.

Leave the cake to cool in the pan for 15 minutes before you unmold it.

ŒUFS
de la Ferme

FROMAGE
vente 7/7

COOKIES

French cookies are bite-size wonders, *petits fours,* which the French serve with coffee at the end of a meal. Most of them are super easy to make and take little time. Some in this chapter are ones adults remember having as children, like the Palets de Dames with Currants or Chocolate Chips (page 72) or Apricot Jam "Eyeglasses" Cookies (page 79). Others are whimsical, like my Eiffel Tower Pie Crust Cookies (page 60). And some are so good you can't stop eating them, like the Giant Break-and-Share Cookie (page 69).

The cookie recipes in this chapter are my favorites, the ones I go to when I want the house filled with cookie goodness. I often make more than one of the recipes and fill a plate with a variety of them. You can never have enough cookies.

EIFFEL TOWER PIE CRUST COOKIES

Biscuits Tour Eiffel QUICKER | AMOUNT VARIES DEPENDING ON COOKIE CUTTER

These have to be the quickest cookies ever. You simply punch them out of store-bought pie crust. Around the holidays I sprinkle them with gold colored sparkling sugar and edible gold leaf. To make them you will need to purchase an Eiffel Tower cookie cutter online.

SPECIAL EQUIPMENT EIFFEL TOWER OR OTHER SHAPE COOKIE CUTTER; 1 BAKING SHEET

Cooking spray

1 package store-bought pie crust

2 tablespoons unsalted butter, melted

1 teaspoon pure vanilla extract

Turbinado or granulated sugar

Colored sugar

Preheat oven to 350 degrees F. Spray the baking sheet with cooking spray.

On a clean floured work surface, roll out the pie crust so that is a uniform thickness and smooth.

Mix the butter with the vanilla extract then brush the pie crust with melted butter and liberally sprinkle with turbinado sugar.

Cut out shapes and place them on the baking sheet. Bake for 10 minutes, until light brown. To decorate, shake colored sugar over the top.

COCONUT DOMES

Congolais **QUICKER** | MAKES 10 DOMES OR 24 SMALL BALLS

I got so addicted to the coconut congolais my local bakery made that were shaped into pyramids and dipped halfway into melted dark chocolate. When they moved away, I began to make them at home. I tried making pyramids but had better luck when I made domes.

My trick to shape these cookies into domes is to tightly pack the coconut mixture into an egg cup and invert onto a baking sheet. If you don't have an egg cup, you can wet your hands and shape them into balls, baking them a minute or two less. They will be light and fluffy, soft on the inside, and crispy on the outside.

Make sure to serve them the same day they are made to preserve the crispy exterior. Use only unsweetened coconut, which you can find in most health food or gourmet stores. It makes a world of difference in how they taste.

SPECIAL EQUIPMENT FOOD PROCESSOR; 2 BAKING SHEETS LINED WITH PARCHMENT PAPER; 1 EGG CUP

Domes

3 cups dried unsweetened shredded coconut

½ cup granulated sugar

⅛ teaspoon salt

1 tablespoon unsalted butter

1 teaspoon pure vanilla extract

1 large egg, room temperature

1 large egg white, room temperature

Drizzle

1 (4-ounce) bittersweet dark chocolate or white chocolate bar, finely chopped

1 teaspoon unsalted butter

DOMES

Preheat oven to 350 degrees F.

Toss the coconut into the food processor with the sugar and salt and process for 10 seconds. Melt butter in the microwave then stir in the vanilla extract.

Whisk the egg and egg white in a large bowl for at least 30 seconds, until they start to turn pale. Pour in the butter mixture and whisk to blend.

Scoop the coconut on top of the egg mixture and, with a whisk, mix really well until every bit of coconut is coated, finishing by using your hands to blend and mix.

To form the domes, rinse the inside of the egg cup with water then pack in the coconut mixture quite tightly. Using a small fork, gently invert the egg cup over the baking sheet and coax the dome out of the cup. Use your fingers to tidy into a nice dome shape. To make the next dome, rinse the inside of the egg cup and repeat. If you are forming small balls, rinse your hands and roll the coconut mixture in the palms of your hands.

Bake the domes for 11 minutes, or until they are golden brown. If you are making small balls, bake them a couple of minutes less, removing from the oven when they are golden. Place the domes or balls on a wire rack and allow to cool to room temperature.

DRIZZLE

If you would like to drizzle or coat the domes with chocolate, melt the chocolate and butter in the microwave then stir until very smooth.

Drizzle the chocolate over the top of the domes with a fork dipped in the chocolate, then refrigerate.

TIPS

Don't melt chocolate chips as they won't work as well or taste as good as bar chocolate. Instead of drizzling, you can dip the tops into the melted chocolate, sprinkle with flakes of coconut or flakes of sea salt, and refrigerate for 30 minutes so the chocolate hardens. Serve the same day.

PUMPKIN SEED TUILES

Tuiles aux Graines de Courge QUICKER | MAKES APPROXIMATELY 14 COOKIES

One of the easiest and fastest cookies to make, tuiles *are traditionally served in France with ice cream or sorbet. They take just minutes to make once you let the batter rest for half an hour. They are crispest the day you make them but are also great right out of the freezer.*

SPECIAL EQUIPMENT 2 BAKING SHEETS; FOOD PROCESSOR; ROLLING PIN

7 heaping tablespoons salted pumpkin seeds, divided

⅓ cup granulated sugar

1 teaspoon finely grated orange zest

3 tablespoons salted butter, room temperature

1 teaspoon pure vanilla extract

2 large egg whites, room temperature

3 tablespoons all-purpose flour

1 tablespoon cornstarch

Preheat oven to 350 degrees F. Place the oven rack in the middle of the oven. Lightly butter and flour the baking sheets.

Place 2 tablespoons pumpkin seeds in the food processor with the sugar and orange zest and process until the pumpkin seeds are finely ground.

Add the butter and process for 1 minute. Scrape down the sides of the processor bowl. Add the vanilla and egg whites and process for about 1 minute. Sprinkle in the flour and cornstarch and pulse just until combined, no longer. Scoop into a bowl and let the batter rest for 30 minutes.

Meanwhile, clean and dry the food processor bowl then process the remaining pumpkin seeds until they form small chunks. Set aside.

To bake the cookies, drop level tablespoons of the batter onto 1 baking sheet, spacing them at least 3 inches apart. With the back of the spoon or a wet finger, gently spread out into thin circles.

Lightly sprinkle the circles with the reserved pumpkin seeds, place in the oven, and bake for 6–10 minutes, until the edges turn light brown. Take out of the oven but keep the oven on.

Work quickly as the cookies will rapidly harden. Use a spatula or palette knife to transfer the cookies from the baking sheet and drape them over the rolling pin before they become too hard. You want them to take on a U shape. I often just use my hands to hold them for a few seconds until they harden into shape, or roll them into cigar shapes.

When they are thoroughly cool and hardened, remove from the rolling pin.

Repeat the process with the second baking sheet as it is not hot from the oven. Keep rotating baking sheets and baking cookies until the dough is finished.

TIP

Form them into cups to hold ice cream or fresh fruit and whipped cream by fitting them into muffin tins while still warm. Also, you can shape them into fortune cookies with individualized fortunes inside.

IRRESISTIBLE ESPRESSO ALMOND COOKIES

Biscuits Irrésistibles à l'Expresso et aux Amandes **QUICKER** | MAKES ABOUT 50 (2- TO 3-INCH) COOKIES

In several regions in France, especially in Nancy, there is a recipe people make for almond cookies that is simply a combination of three ingredients: ground almonds, sugar, and egg whites. I found that if I add a dose of instant espresso powder, they are irresistible dunked into espresso after a meal.

SPECIAL EQUIPMENT FOOD PROCESSOR; 2 BAKING SHEETS LINED WITH PARCHMENT PAPER

1 cup whole almonds	1 cup granulated sugar	4 large egg whites, room temperature
3 cups almond flour	¼ teaspoon salt	
1 tablespoon plus 1 teaspoon instant espresso powder	3 tablespoons light brown sugar	1 teaspoon almond extract
		½ teaspoon pure vanilla extract

Preheat oven to 350 degrees F.

Add the whole almonds, almond flour, espresso powder, granulated sugar, salt, brown sugar, egg whites, and almond and vanilla extracts to the bowl of a food processor and process until you have a paste.

Using a tablespoon, drop spoonfuls of the paste onto a baking sheet to make the cookies, spacing them 1 inch apart. Wet your fingers and gently tap the top of the cookies to smooth and flatten them out to even circles of about 2–3 inches across.

Bake for 15 minutes, until the edges turn light brown. Repeat the process to use up the batter on the second cool baking sheet. If needed, keep rotating baking sheets until all the cookies are made. Cool on a wire rack.

GIANT BREAK-AND-SHARE COOKIE

Le Broyé du Poitou **QUICKER** | MAKES 1 COOKIE

In 2004 a group called the La Confrérie de l'Ordre des Chevaliers de la Grand Goule formed to protect and promote the tradition of making of this giant cookie, a specialty of the Poitou-Charentes region of France. It's a cookie worth protecting and promoting.

Recognizable by its criss-cross pattern made with a fork across the top, and by its great size, it is a communal cookie, brought out for people to share after mass, baptisms, weddings, community dinners, and even inaugurations. Once I heard about it, I had to try to find a recipe. This one is adapted from the official recipe on the Confrérie's web site.

I can't stop eating it, and I have to admit it may be my favorite cookie of all time. It tastes a lot like shortbread, and is great dipped into tea or with a glass of milk.

SPECIAL EQUIPMENT FOOD PROCESSOR; 1 BAKING SHEET

3 ¾ cups sifted all-purpose flour

1 ¼ cups granulated sugar

½ teaspoon salt

2 sticks plus 2 tablespoons salted chilled butter, cut into small cubes

1 large egg

3 tablespoons dark rum

1 large egg yolk

Preheat the oven to 350 degrees F.

Place the flour, sugar, and salt in the bowl of a food processor and pulse 6 times.

Add the butter and process until the mixture is granular in texture. Whisk the egg and rum in a small bowl, add to the food processor, and process just until a ball forms. If it is still too dry to form a ball, add 1 tablespoon of ice water at a time until it comes together into a ball.

Place the dough on a large piece of plastic wrap. Press it down into a circle with the palms of your hands. Transfer to the baking sheet, removing and discarding the plastic wrap, and continue shaping and pressing the disk until it is ½ inch thick and approximately 10–11 inches across. Pinch all the way around the edges to create a decorative wave pattern.

Beat the egg yolk and brush it across the top and down the sides. Drag the tines of a fork from one end to the other several times to create a large criss-cross pattern.

Bake for 25–35 minutes, until golden brown. Allow to cool for at least 20 minutes on the baking sheet then carefully slip it off onto a large round plate.

To serve, present the whole cookie and let people break off pieces like they do in Poitiers.

TIP

Some families scatter slivered almonds over the top before baking. You can also form this dough into mini or individual ½-inch-thick cookies if you wish.

CHOCOLATE SABLES

Sablés au Chocolat **QUICKER** | MAKES 25 (3-INCH) COOKIES

Sablés, *buttery cookies from the Normandy region of France, are great just plain vanilla. I make mine with a punch of dark cocoa for a twist on the traditional cookie. These are crunchy and crumbly, with an intense chocolate flavor.*

SPECIAL EQUIPMENT ELECTRIC STAND MIXER; ROLLING PIN; 1 BAKING SHEET LINED WITH PARCHMENT PAPER; ROUND COOKIE CUTTER

2 cups all-purpose flour

½ cup plus 2 tablespoons Hershey's Special Dark Cocoa

¼ teaspoon salt

2 sticks unsalted butter, softened

¼ cup confectioner's sugar

½ cup plus 1 tablespoon granulated sugar

1 ½ teaspoons pure vanilla extract

1 egg white beaten with 1 teaspoon water

Crystallized or turbinado sugar

Sift the flour and cocoa together into a mixing bowl. Add the salt and whisk together.

Beat the butter, confectioner's sugar, and granulated sugar with the mixer for 4 minutes, scraping down the sides of the bowl a couple of times. Add the vanilla and beat to combine. Pour in the flour mixture and mix just until combined, without overmixing.

Scoop the dough out onto a large sheet of plastic wrap, form into a ball and place another sheet of plastic wrap on top. Use the palms of your hands to flatten, and with the rolling pin, roll the dough out to ¼ inch thick. Refrigerate for 30 minutes.

Preheat oven to 350 degrees F.

Use a cookie cutter or a glass to cut out round cookies. Lay cookies on the baking sheet, brush them with the egg wash, sprinkle generously with crystallized sugar for a nice crunchy top, and bake for 13–15 minutes, until crisp. Remove from the oven, cool on the baking sheet for a couple of minutes, then transfer to a wire rack.

LAUGHING COW SUGAR COOKIES

Biscuits à la Vache qui Rit **QUICKER** | MAKES ABOUT 36 TO 40 (2-INCH) COOKIES

These delicate crisp little cookies have a secret ingredient—Laughing Cow Swiss cheese. I learned to use Laughing Cow cheese as a substitute for cream cheese in American recipes when I lived in France. It works beautifully. The cookies have a luxurious taste and feel, reminiscent of the cream cheese cookies my grandmother used to make.

SPECIAL EQUIPMENT ELECTRIC HAND MIXER; 2 BAKING SHEETS LINED WITH PARCHMENT PAPER

1 stick unsalted butter, room temperature

4 wedges Laughing Cow Swiss cheese, room temperature

½ teaspoon pure vanilla extract

½ cup plus 1 tablespoon granulated sugar

1 cup all-purpose flour

1 egg white, lightly beaten

Turbinado sugar

Preheat oven to 375 degrees F.

In a mixing bowl, add the butter, cheese wedges, and vanilla and beat with the mixer until combined. Pour in the sugar and beat until combined.

Pour in the flour and beat well to combine until the dough is smooth, scraping the sides of the bowl once or twice.

Drop by generously rounded teaspoons onto the baking sheets, leaving 2 inches between each cookie. Flatten each by tapping and rounding with your finger into 1- to 2- inch circles. Moisten your finger in the egg white and rub gently in circles over the

top of each cookie to smooth the tops and edges. Dab with more egg white then generously sprinkle turbinado sugar over the top of each cookie.

Bake for 7–10 minutes, until the edges are golden brown. Remove from the oven, cool for 2 minutes, then remove to a plate or cooling rack and repeat with the remaining dough.

TIP

If you are baking these cookies for the holidays, instead of topping with turbinado sugar, sprinkle on some festive colored sugar or sprinkles.

PALETS DE DAMES WITH CURRANTS OR CHOCOLATE CHIPS

Palets de Dames aux Raisins Secs ou aux Pépites de Chocolat

QUICKER | MAKES 6 CURRANT COOKIES AND 6 CHOCOLATE CHIP COOKIES

A specialty of northern France, some palets de dames *cookies are frosted, some are not, and some are thinner than others, but for the most part, they all contain rum-soaked currants. This recipe is divided in half, which will result in half of the cookies having rum-soaked currants and the other half of the cookies having mini chocolate chips.*

SPECIAL EQUIPMENT ELECTRIC STAND MIXER; 2 BAKING SHEETS LINED WITH PARCHMENT PAPER

Cookies

¼ cup plus 2 tablespoons rum

5 tablespoons currants

1 stick unsalted butter, softened

½ cup plus 3 tablespoons confectioner's sugar

½ teaspoon pure vanilla extract

2 large eggs, room temperature

1 cup all-purpose flour

¼ teaspoon baking soda

3 tablespoons mini chocolate chips

Glaze

1 cup confectioner's sugar

2 tablespoons plus 1 teaspoon rum

COOKIES

Preheat the oven to 400 degrees F.

Heat the rum in a saucepan until it just begins to bubble around the edges. Toss in the currants and cook for 1 minute. Turn off the heat and let them soak for 10 minutes then drain off the liquid and discard.

Using the mixer, beat the butter and sugar together for about 2 minutes. Add the vanilla and beat to combine. Beat in the eggs, one at a time. Sift in the flour and baking soda and stir to combine. Divide the dough in half and place in separate bowls.

Add 4 tablespoons of currants to 1 bowl and the mini chocolate chips to the other bowl. Stir to combine both batches.

Drop the batter in rounded tablespoons onto the baking sheets, at least 2 inches apart. Wet your fingers and gently tap into circles with slightly rounded tops. Gently press some of the remaining currants onto the tops of each of the currant-filled cookies.

Bake all the cookies for 7–9 minutes, until they just begin to turn golden.

GLAZE

Use a fork to mix the confectioner's sugar and rum into a thick paste. Brush the glaze over the top of the currant cookies while they are still hot. The glaze will start to melt and you can even it out into a smooth glaze. Allow the glaze to harden before serving.

Lightly dust the chocolate chip cookies with confectioner's sugar after they have cooled.

ANISE COOKIES WITH PISTACHIOS AND DRIED CHERRIES

La Cornuelle Charentaise aux Pistaches et aux Cerises Séchées

QUICKER | MAKES ABOUT 20 COOKIES

In the area of Charentes in the western part of central France, there is a special triangular cookie made and eaten on Palm Sunday. It is buttery, has ruffled edges, and an unusual hole in the center. Why three sided? Some say it is to represent the Father, the Son, and the Holy Ghost. Why the hole? I have sometimes seen them threaded through a twig to represent a tree when all stacked up.

These cookies are normally sprinkled with anise seeds, but I have also added drops of anise extract to further enhance their traditional flavor, and I like to include pistachios and dried cherries to add interest. I cut out a triangle from parchment paper then lay it over the dough to cut the shapes, not bothering to cut a circle out of each unless I want to string them on ribbon for Christmas swags.

SPECIAL EQUIPMENT MORTAR AND PESTLE OR SPICE GRINDER; ELECTRIC HAND MIXER; 1 (2- TO 3-INCH) TRIANGLE SHAPE TEMPLATE CUT OUT OF PARCHMENT PAPER; 1 BAKING SHEET

2 teaspoons anise seeds, plus more to garnish	1/4 teaspoon salt	1/4 teaspoon baking powder
1/4 cup shelled salted pistachios	1 teaspoon pure anise extract	1/4 cup dried cherries, coarsely chopped
2 sticks unsalted butter, room temperature	1/2 teaspoon pure vanilla extract	1 egg yolk beaten with 1 teaspoon milk
3/4 cup confectioner's sugar	1 large egg	
	2 cups all-purpose flour	Turbinado or granulated sugar

Lightly grind 2 teaspoons anise seeds in a mortar and pestle or spice grinder. Leave the seeds for garnish whole or lightly chop. Toast the pistachios for about 2 minutes in a dry pan, cool, then coarsely chop. Reserve for garnish.

Slice butter into a large bowl. With the mixer, beat the butter with the confectioner's sugar, salt, ground anise seeds, anise and vanilla extracts, and the egg.

Sift the flour and baking powder together then add this to the butter mixture, 1 cup at a time, mixing with a wooden spoon until a dough forms. Wrap the dough in a piece of plastic wrap, flatten into a disk, and refrigerate for 1 hour.

Preheat oven to 350 degrees F.

On a clean sugared work surface, roll out the dough to about 1/2 inch thick. If it crumbles, use your fingers to repair. Place the triangular piece of parchment paper over the dough, slice triangles of dough, and place them on an ungreased baking sheet.

Press pistachios and cherries onto the tops of each cookie in an attractive pattern. Brush the tops with the egg wash, sprinkle on a little turbinado sugar, then scatter with some anise seeds.

Place in the oven and bake for 18–20 minutes, until lightly browned. Remove from oven and cool.

LITTLE BOAT COOKIES FROM MARSEILLE

Les Navettes Marseillaises **QUICKER** | MAKES 12 COOKIES

Shaped like little rowboats, navettes *are small unadorned cookies scented with orange flower water and, along with* crêpes, *are required fare during the Christian holiday of Candlemas every February 2nd. It is said that the cookies were shaped to symbolize the small boat that carried Mary Magdalene to the fishing village of Saintes-Maries-de-la-Mer in Provence. Enjoy them dipped into coffee or tea.*

SPECIAL EQUIPMENT 1 BAKING SHEET LINED WITH PARCHMENT PAPER

2 ¾ cups all-purpose flour

1 ½ teaspoons baking powder

½ teaspoon salt

2 large eggs

1 teaspoon orange extract

5 tablespoons olive oil

1 cup plus 2 tablespoons confectioner's sugar

1 tablespoon finely grated organic orange zest

Preheat the oven to 400 degrees F.

Sift the flour, baking powder, and salt into a large mixing bowl.

With a fork, beat the eggs with the orange extract and olive oil and add this mixture to the bowl. Add the sugar and orange zest and stir with a wooden spoon until it is well combined.

Flour your hands and work the dough until it is smooth and comes together. Flour the dough, if needed, and roll it into a log. Slice the dough into pieces as large as you would like your cookies to be.

Flour your hands and roll each piece into an oval then pinch the ends to make it resemble a small boat. Use a dull knife to gently press down the center of each to create an indentation in the middle. Bake for 20–25 minutes, until they just turn golden.

ORANGE MADELEINES WITH ORANGE GLAZE

Les Madeleines Glacées à l'Orange **LONGER** | MAKES 24 MADELEINES

"And suddenly the memory revealed itself. The taste was that of the little piece of madeleine which on Sunday mornings at Combray (because on those mornings I did not go out before mass), when I went to say good morning to her in her bedroom, my aunt Léonie used to give me, dipping it first in her own cup of tea or tisane."— Marcel Proust, In Search of Lost Time

Although technically not a cookie, I serve these small shell-shaped cakes like I would cookies, with tea or coffee after dinner. Madeleine baking pans have scallop-shaped indentations that give them their unique shape. If you don't have one, use mini muffin tins to make buttery, soft mini cakes

A specialty of Commercy in northeastern France, madeleines became popular with Louis XV's court at Versailles, and later became popular all over France.

SPECIAL EQUIPMENT CITRUS MICROPLANE; 2 MADELEINE BAKING TINS OR 1 MINI MUFFIN PAN

Madeleines

1 organic orange, microplaned for zest then juiced

2 large eggs

1 large egg yolk

½ cup granulated sugar

1 teaspoon pure vanilla extract

1 cup cake flour

1 teaspoon baking powder

1 stick salted butter, melted and still warm

Glaze

¾ cup confectioner's sugar

Enough orange juice to make spreadable glaze

MADELEINES

Divide the orange zest into 2 piles.

Make the batter by hand, not using an electric mixer, to ensure tender madeleines. In a large mixing bowl, whisk together the eggs, egg yolk, and sugar to combine. Whisk in half of the orange zest, vanilla, and 1 teaspoon orange juice. Sift in the flour and baking powder and stir to just combine.

Pour in the butter and whisk to just combine. Cover with plastic wrap and refrigerate for 1 hour.

Preheat oven to 375 degrees F. Butter and flour the madeleine tins and put them in the freezer until ready to use so that the butter hardens.

Pour the batter into the madeleine tins until just filled, trying for a mound in the center. If you are making large madeleines, they will take 14–16 minutes to bake until puffed and golden brown on top. Small ones will take approximately 8–10 minutes. Cool in pans for 2 minutes before removing.

GLAZE

Mix the confectioner's sugar with just enough orange juice to make an opaque, thick, yet spreadable glaze. Spread over each Madeleine with a pastry brush, sprinkle the remaining orange zest over the tops, and allow to dry for about 20 minutes before serving.

BRETON BUTTER COOKIES

Les Palets Bretons **LONGER** | MAKES 25 COOKIES

Round and fat, thick and crumbly, palets *are slightly salty and sweet butter cookies traditionally made with butter from Brittany. Cookie making is big business in Brittany, with many cookie factories churning out buttery renditions of* palets *packaged in festive tin boxes, the prettiest of which I think are the Quimper tins decorated in the style of the plates from the same region.*

SPECIAL EQUIPMENT FOOD PROCESSOR; 1 BAKING SHEET LINED WITH PARCHMENT PAPER

½ **cup salted butter, softened**

¼ **cup granulated sugar**

¼ **cup light brown sugar**

1 ½ **teaspoons pure vanilla extract**

2 **large egg yolks**

1 ½ **cups all-purpose flour**

1 **teaspoon baking powder**

Slice the butter into the food processor then add the granulated and brown sugars, vanilla, and egg yolks; process to combine. Sift the flour and baking powder together then add to the food processor and process until a dough ball forms.

Sprinkle granulated sugar over a clean work surface. Make a round ball of the dough then, using your hands, roll out the dough into a long log, about 1 ½ inches in diameter. As you form the log, make sure to press into the sugar to give it a nice crust on the outside. Slice the log in half, wrap both pieces in plastic wrap, and refrigerate for 2 hours.

Preheat oven to 350 degrees F.

Slice the dough logs into ½-inch-thick circles, place on the baking sheet, and bake for 11–12 minutes, until golden brown. Cool to room temperature before serving.

APRICOT JAM "EYEGLASSES" COOKIES

Les Lunettes à la Confiture **LONGER** | MAKES ABOUT 12 (3-INCH) COOKIES

I used to see these all the time in my village's pastry shop, little jam cookies with two small circles cut out to resemble eyeglasses. Lunettes is French for eyeglasses. If you have fluted oval cookie cutters, they will look like traditional lunettes cookies when you make them. Dust the tops with confectioner's sugar and enjoy!

SPECIAL EQUIPMENT ELECTRIC STAND MIXER; OVAL COOKIE CUTTER; 1 BAKING SHEET LINED WITH PARCHMENT PAPER

1 ½ sticks unsalted butter, room temperature

¾ cup plus 2 tablespoons granulated sugar

1 organic lemon, zested then juiced

1 teaspoon pure vanilla extract

2 eggs, lightly beaten

2 cups all-purpose flour

½ cup cornstarch

¼ teaspoon salt

½ cup apricot jam

Confectioner's sugar

Slice the butter into the bowl of the mixer and beat until pale and thick, about 2 minutes. Add the sugar and lemon zest and beat for 5 minutes, until fluffy. Add 1 teaspoon lemon juice, vanilla, and eggs and beat to combine.

Sift the flour, cornstarch, and salt together then add it to the bowl and beat only until it is combined and you have a soft sticky dough. Scoop out onto a large piece of plastic wrap, form into a ball, flatten into a disk, and refrigerate for 1 hour.

Preheat oven to 350 degrees F.

Dust the dough disk on both sides with flour. Put the dough disk between 2 pieces of parchment paper and roll out to ⅛ inch thick. Cut out all of the cookies with the cookie cutter then, in half of them, cut 2 small circles to make the "eyeglasses." Place all the cookies on the baking sheet and bake for 5 minutes then turn the baking sheet to rotate them and cook

for another 5 minutes, just until the cookies begin to turn golden along the edges. Remove from the oven and allow to cool.

Heat the jam gently until it melts and loosens, cool to room temperature, and spread 2 teaspoons onto the cookies without holes, not quite to the edges. Liberally dust the ones with holes with confectioner's sugar then place them on top of each one with jam and press lightly so the jam just begins to emerge from the holes.

TIP

Why not try peanut butter and jelly? Or lemon curd? On Valentine's Day, cut out hearts instead of eyeglasses, at Christmas cut out trees. Make them with different colors and flavors of jam.

BAKED

There's nostalgia attached to baking that comes from the wonderful aromas filling a kitchen while making bread or cake or cookies, reminding us of our childhood. I especially love to bake because of this. My instant mood booster is to go into the kitchen to bake.

Some of these recipes were created with company in mind; some with nothing more in mind than wanting to bring a comforting dessert to the table to share with the family.

FRESH FRUIT PAPILLOTES WITH MELTING ICE CREAM

Papillotes de Fruits Frais et Glace Fondante **QUICKER** | SERVES 4

En papillote, cooking in a paper packet, means that you can cook without butter and produce intense flavors and natural juices from the steam that builds inside. It's one of the easiest cooking methods and works beautifully for fresh fruit desserts. Approach this recipe with abandon, picking any seasonal fruit you may find and adding in fresh herbs from your garden if you wish.

I scoop balls of vanilla ice cream into a large bowl and keep it in the freezer until my packets arrive on the table. Each person will have their own packet of seasonal fruit. As they unfurl the paper packet, the aroma of warm fruit fills the air. Then the bowl of ice cream balls is passed to each person so they can place one on top of their hot fruit, where it melts, creating a cool vanilla sauce.

SPECIAL EQUIPMENT FOOD PROCESSOR; CITRUS MICROPLANE; 4 (14 X 14-INCH) PIECES OF PARCHMENT PAPER; 1 BAKING SHEET

2 tablespoons granulated sugar	1 large organic orange	12 large strawberries
2 tablespoons light brown sugar	2 kiwis	2 cups mixed berries (raspberries, blueberries, and blackberries)
1 vanilla bean	1 peach	Confectioner's sugar
¼ teaspoon ground cinnamon	2 bananas	1 quart vanilla ice cream

Place the granulated and brown sugars into the bowl of the food processor. Slice the vanilla bean in half vertically and scrape the seeds into the bowl on top of the sugar. Save the bean pod for later. Add the cinnamon and process for 10 seconds. Scoop into a mixing bowl.

Using the microplane, zest the orange into the bowl. Use a sharp knife to cut away the remaining peel and white pith from the orange, slice it thinly, and toss into the bowl.

Peel and slice the kiwis and toss them into the bowl. Slice the peach in eighths and add to the bowl. Peel the bananas, slice into ⅛-inch slices, and toss into the bowl. Slice the strawberries in half, place in the bowl, and toss in the mixed berries.

Stir everything gently to coat and let set for 20 minutes while you preheat the oven to 400 degrees F.

Working on a long counter or table, lay out the 4 pieces of parchment paper into an assembly line.

Evenly divide the fruit onto the middle of each piece of paper, drizzling any juices at the bottom of the bowl over the top of each pile. Slice the vanilla pod into 4 pieces and lay a piece over the top of each pile.

To make the packets, bring together the paper horizontally and fold it down to almost touch the fruit below, fold and twist the ends, and fold them under the packet. Place the packets on the baking sheet. You want them to be a size that will fit on a dessert plate.

Bake for 20 minutes, or until the packets puff up. Leave on the baking sheet for 15 minutes then transfer each packet to a dessert plate and lightly dust with confectioner's sugar. Allow people to open their own packet, and then pass scoops of ice cream for them to place on top and melt over the hot fruit. A little bowl of whipped cream doesn't hurt either.

TIP

Opening the packets before bringing them to the table and scattering fresh edible flowers or fresh herbs over the top of the fruit makes a stunning presentation.

PEACH FLAUGNARDE

Flaugnarde aux Pêches **QUICKER** | SERVES 6

A clafoutis is only made with fresh cherries. When using any other fruits, it is called a flaugnarde. *But the two are similar in every other way. When I load up the car with sweet, ripe peaches from the farmers market, I head home and make this dessert for dinner. It's quick to prepare and beautifully highlights the fresh peaches.*

SPECIAL EQUIPMENT 1 (8-CUP) BAKING DISH

1 pound fresh peaches, sliced, or 1 (16-ounce) package frozen sliced peaches

½ cup plus 6 tablespoons granulated sugar, divided

5 tablespoons whiskey, divided

3 large eggs, room temperature

¼ teaspoon salt

2 teaspoons pure vanilla extract

½ cup all-purpose flour

3⁄4 cup plus 2 tablespoons half-and-half

4 tablespoons melted butter

Preheat oven to 350 degrees F. Generously butter the baking dish and flour the sides.

Bring the peaches, 3 tablespoons sugar, and 3 tablespoons whiskey to a simmer in a saucepan and cook for 5 minutes. Drain the peaches and spoon them into the bottom of the baking dish. Discard any liquid.

In a large mixing bowl, whisk the eggs, ½ cup sugar, salt, and vanilla together to combine. Add the flour and half-and-half and whisk to combine. Pour in the butter and remaining whiskey and whisk well.

Pour this mixture over the fruit and bake for 35 minutes, or until set. Take out of the oven, sprinkle the top with the remaining sugar, and return to the oven to bake for 7 minutes.

Take out of the oven and allow to rest for 10–15 minutes before cutting into serving pieces. The flaugnarde will deflate, so don't worry how it looks. It will be a delicious, comforting dessert that will taste even better with a scoop of ice cream on top to melt over the peaches.

BAKED BANANA AND CHOCOLATE PAIN PERDU

Pain Perdu au Four à la Banane et au Chocolat QUICKER | SERVES 8

I've seen pain perdu *served in French restaurants as one slice topped with berries and confectioner's sugar, and I've seen it in homes baked in small individual ramekins filled with little chunks of bread into a dessert resembling more of an American bread pudding. I prefer making it in a large baking dish then spooning it into dessert bowls or ramekins.*

SPECIAL EQUIPMENT 1 BAKING SHEET; 1 (9-INCH) ROUND OR SQUARE BAKING PAN AT LEAST 2 INCHES DEEP; 1 ROASTING PAN; 8 RAMEKINS OR SERVING BOWLS

1 unsliced loaf white bread, challah, or soft Italian bread

¾ cup granulated sugar

5 large egg yolks

2 large eggs

2 tablespoons rum

2 teaspoons pure vanilla extract

¼ teaspoon salt

2 ½ cups half-and-half

4 ripe bananas, divided

2 tablespoons unsalted butter, melted

1 (8-ounce) semisweet chocolate bar, finely chopped

Confectioner's sugar

Preheat oven to 300 degrees F.

Cut 9 slices of bread from the loaf, making them each 1 inch thick. Stack them and slice off the crusts. Cut each slice of bread into 1–inch cubes. Spread them out in 1 layer on the baking sheet, place in the oven, and bake for 8 minutes to dry out and crisp the bread. Remove from the oven but leave the oven on.

Generously butter the baking dish.

In a large mixing bowl, whisk together the sugar, egg yolks, eggs, rum, vanilla, and salt to combine. Add the half-and-half and whisk well. Slice 3 of the bananas into the mixture, making them about ¼ inch thick.

Scoop the toasted bread into the mixing bowl, gently toss to coat, and let set for 5 minutes.

Pour this mixture into the baking dish and use a pastry brush to coat the bread that peeks up with melted butter. Slice the remaining banana and arrange the slices decoratively over the top then place the dish into the roasting pan.

Fill the roasting pan halfway up with hot water and bake in the center of the oven for 40 minutes. Sprinkle the chocolate over the top and bake for another 20 minutes, until the chocolate has melted and the custard below is set. Touch the center with the back of a spoon. If custard seeps out, you need to cook it a little longer.

Bring to the table and serve into individual ramekins with a sprinkle of confectioner's sugar.

TIP

If you like raisins, try soaking them in rum for 10 minutes and adding them to the pain perdu instead of bananas and chocolate. Do not use chocolate chips as the bar of chocolate melts much better.

ROASTED PEACHES IN A POOL OF CRÈME ANGLAISE

Pêches Rôties et Crème Anglaise **QUICKER** | SERVES 4

Roasting peaches brings out their beautiful aroma and flavor. I serve these warm out of the oven in a pool of chilled crème anglaise with a few small thyme leaves to garnish for an elegant summer dessert.

SPECIAL EQUIPMENT ELECTRIC HAND MIXER; 1 BAKING DISH TO HOLD 8 PEACH HALVES

Crème Anglaise

2 cups half-and-half

2 tablespoons honey

3 star anise

4 large egg yolks, room temperature

¼ cup plus 2 tablespoons granulated sugar

1 tablespoon light brown sugar

1 teaspoon pure vanilla extract

Peaches

½ cup water

½ cup granulated sugar

8 sprigs fresh thyme, divided

4 large peaches

CRÈME ANGLAISE

Make the custard sauce by pouring the half-and-half, honey, and star anise into a medium saucepan and cook over medium heat until the honey has melted. Allow to simmer for 3 minutes then remove and discard the star anise.

Using the mixer, beat the egg yolks, granulated sugar, and brown sugar for about 4 minutes. Then, while beating on low speed, slowly pour in ½ cup of the hot half-and-half mixture and beat to combine. Pour this back into the saucepan and cook over medium-low heat, constantly whisking or stirring, until the custard coats the back of a spoon and is slightly thickened.

Take off the heat, cool to room temperature, whisk in the vanilla, cover with plastic wrap touching the custard, and refrigerate until ready to use.

PEACHES

To make thyme-scented simple syrup, put the water and sugar in a saucepan, bring to a boil, throw in 6 sprigs of thyme, lower the heat, and simmer for 7 minutes. Remove and discard the thyme.

Preheat oven to 350 degrees F. Generously butter the baking dish, and bring a pot of water to boil.

Plunge peaches into boiling water for 5 seconds, run under cold water, peel, then slice in half and remove and discard the pits.

Place the peach halves in the baking dish with the cut side up, pour the thyme syrup into the hollow of each peach, and bake for 15–20 minutes. Begin checking at 10 minutes. You want the peaches to cook yet still have form and a bit of a bite.

To serve, spoon a pool of Crème Anglaise on each plate and place 2 warm halves of peaches on the top. Drizzle with any juices left in the baking dish and garnish with the tiny leaves from the remaining thyme.

TIP

If you are in a hurry, melt some vanilla bean ice cream in the microwave and serve it in a small pitcher to pour over the warm peaches instead of making the Crème Anglaise.

INDIVIDUAL BERRIES GRATIN WITH YOGURT WHIPPED CREAM

Gratins Individuels aux Fruits Rouges, Crème Fouettée au Yaourt QUICKER | SERVES 4

My girlfriend Nathalie makes her summer fruit gratins with yogurt, and the tang of it against the berries and topping is sublime. I took her cue and created a recipe with summer berries, serving it, like she does, with sweetened whipped cream mixed with a little yogurt.

SPECIAL EQUIPMENT 4 INDIVIDUAL GRATIN DISHES OR RAMEKINS; 1 ROASTING PAN OR BAKING SHEET; ELECTRIC HAND MIXER

Gratin

1 pound mixed berries, plus extra to garnish

$\frac{1}{2}$ cup superfine sugar

1 cup plain Greek yogurt

2 large eggs

1 teaspoon pure vanilla extract

4 tablespoons granulated sugar

$\frac{1}{2}$ teaspoon almond extract

2 tablespoons all-purpose flour

Confectioner's sugar

Whipped Cream

1 cup heavy whipping cream, chilled

$\frac{1}{2}$ cup plain Greek yogurt

3 tablespoons granulated sugar

1 teaspoon pure vanilla extract

GRATIN

Preheat oven to 350 degrees F. Butter and sugar the gratin dishes.

Add the berries to a mixing bowl, pour the superfine sugar over the top, and gently mix with your hands to coat. Divide the berries between the dishes and place the dishes in a roasting pan.

In a separate mixing bowl, whisk together the yogurt, eggs, vanilla, granulated sugar, and almond extract until well combined. Sift in the flour and whisk to combine. Pour this mixture over the berries and bake for 25–35 minutes, until golden brown.

WHIPPED CREAM

Using the hand mixer, beat all the ingredients together until soft mounds form.

Serve the gratins warm with a light dusting of confectioner's sugar, a dollop of whipped yogurt cream, and a few fresh berries scattered on top.

TIP

You can make this with frozen raspberries if needed, just don't thaw them before baking.

SWEET SUGAR BREAD ARDENNAISE

Tarte au Sucre Ardennaise **LONGER** | SERVES 4

A sense of serenity falls upon me when I make this bread. I reserve it for the weekends when I can sit down in the silence of the afternoon, brew tea, open preserves I made in the summer, and treat myself to a slice. It comes from the region of Ardennes in northern France. Most of the recipes on blogs and in French cooking magazines are virtually identical for the bread, and this is the sum of those recipes.

SPECIAL EQUIPMENT 1 (9-INCH) PIE PLATE

Bread

2 ⅔ cups all-purpose flour

¼ cup plus 2 tablespoons granulated sugar

¼ teaspoon salt

1 packet plus ½ teaspoon active dry yeast

2 large eggs, room temperature

½ cup milk, room temperature

1 stick unsalted butter, melted

1 teaspoon pure vanilla extract or orange flower water

Topping

1 egg

¼ cup granulated sugar, divided

BREAD

Add the flour, sugar, salt, and yeast to a large mixing bowl and whisk to combine.

Whisk the eggs into the milk, add the melted butter and vanilla, and whisk well.

Pour the wet ingredients into the dry ingredients and use a spoon to mix into a smooth dough. Sprinkle it with some flour and, with your hands, begin to knead it in the bowl for 5 minutes, sprinkling more flour as needed to keep it from being sticky.

Cover with plastic wrap without the wrap touching the dough, cover with a towel, place on a kitchen counter or in a warm place, and allow to rise for at least 2 hours or more.

Preheat oven to 375 degrees F. Butter and flour the pie plate.

Place the dough in the pie plate and press down gently in the middle to make a shallow well to hold the topping.

TOPPING

Beat the egg with 2 tablespoons sugar and pour this into the well in the center of the dough, sprinkling the remaining sugar all over the top. Place in the oven and bake for 20–25 minutes, until golden brown. Serve warm.

PUFFS WITH WARM CHOCOLATE SAUCE

Choux à la Crème, Sauce Tiède au Chocolat **LONGER** | MAKES 14 TO 20 PUFFS

Although cream puffs look hard to make, they are anything but. Try them. Once you master them, you can go on to make the famous towering cake called croquembouche, which is simply lots of puffs held together with caramel in a pyramid as high as you want to make it. For now, present three in a row on each dessert plate then drizzle with chocolate sauce.

SPECIAL EQUIPMENT 1 BAKING SHEET

Puffs

$\frac{1}{2}$ cup water

$\frac{1}{2}$ cup milk

1 stick unsalted butter

3 tablespoons confectioner's sugar

2 teaspoons granulated sugar

$\frac{1}{4}$ teaspoon salt

1 $\frac{1}{2}$ teaspoons pure vanilla extract

1 cup all-purpose flour

4 large eggs, room temperature

1 large egg yolk beaten with 1 teaspoon water

Turbinado sugar or crystallized sugar

1 can real whipped cream

Chocolate Sauce

1 cup half-and-half

$\frac{1}{2}$ cup light corn syrup

$\frac{1}{4}$ cup plus 2 tablespoons confectioner's sugar

1 cup Hershey's Special Dark Cocoa

PUFFS

In a large saucepan, bring the water, milk, butter, confectioner's sugar, granulated sugar, and salt to a simmer. When the butter is completely melted, add the vanilla and stir.

Turn heat down to low, add all of the flour, and vigorously stir to combine. Continue to stir until the dough pulls away from the sides of the pan. Scoop this dough into a mixing bowl and allow to cool for 5 minutes.

Vigorously beat in 1 egg at a time until the dough becomes shiny and very smooth.

Cover with plastic wrap and refrigerate for 35 minutes, or more, while you preheat the oven to 400 degrees F.

Either pipe the dough onto the baking sheet or use a small ice cream scoop to shape small balls and place on the sheet, leaving some space in between them. Coat your finger with melted butter or water

and gently coax each one into a round ball shape. Brush with the egg wash and sprinkle with turbinado sugar.

Bake for 20–23 minutes, until the puffs are golden. Turn the oven off, crack open the door, and leave them in the oven for 10 minutes.

To fill, slip the nozzle of the can of whipped cream into each one and fill. Place them in the refrigerator until ready to use.

CHOCOLATE SAUCE

Make the chocolate sauce by pouring all of the ingredients into a saucepan and whisking while it cooks on medium until it forms small bubbles around the edges and is thoroughly melted and smooth. If it needs to be thinned out, add water, 1 tablespoon at a time.

To serve, divide the puffs between dessert plates and drizzle them with the warm chocolate sauce.

FAR BRETON PRUNE CUSTARD CAKE

Le Far Breton **LONGER** | SERVES 10 TO 12

When I first visited Brittany, it was a bitterly cold day swept by rumbling winds and rain. I took refuge in a small café and ordered an espresso and a slice of Far Breton—a custard cake so solid and compact you can carry it in your hands and eat it on the street. All Far Bretons have prunes, and mine was packed with ones that had been soaked in Armagnac, juicy and wonderful against the egg custard.

The rain stopped and I strolled through a few shops where I found an antique serving spoon with a Celtic design. I thought back to my slice of Far Breton, and decided to buy the spoon to make beautiful designs with confectioner's sugar over the top of the Far I would make when I returned home. The spoon makes the design you see in the photograph if I lay it flat and sift confectioner's sugar over it. You can do the same with any cake server or flat utensil with cut-out work, or even with a paper doily.

SPECIAL EQUIPMENT 1 (9- OR 10-INCH) BAKING DISH

4 cups whole milk, room temperature	**1 teaspoon almond extract**	**14 ounces pitted prunes**
4 large eggs	**1 ½ cups granulated sugar**	**Confectioner's sugar**
4 tablespoons salted butter, melted	**2 cups flour**	
	2 tablespoons salted butter	

In a large mixing bowl, whisk the milk, eggs, melted butter, almond extract, and granulated sugar until combined. Gradually add in the flour and vigorously whisk until you have a smooth batter consistency. Let rest for 1 hour.

After 45 minutes have passed, generously butter the baking dish then add 2 tablespoons butter cut into pieces in the bottom. Place the baking dish in a cold oven and set the oven to 400 degrees F.

You want the butter in the baking dish to turn a light brown and smell nutty. Sometimes this takes 10 minutes or less, sometimes 15 minutes, depending on the oven, so check every 5 minutes. It ideally should coincide with when the oven reaches 400 degrees F.

When the oven reaches 400 degrees F, take the baking dish out and slice or cut the prunes in half and arrange them across the bottom of the dish. Pour the batter over the fruit and bake for 15 minutes. Reduce the oven heat to 350 degrees F and bake for another 40–50 minutes, until a knife in the center comes out clean.

Allow to cool to room temperature and slice into squares to serve. I like serving mine warm, but it is equally good chilled. Decorate with sifted confectioner's sugar.

TIP

If you would like, you can swap out the prunes and use a combination of peaches and raspberries or apple and pear chunks or apricots.

CEDRATS CONFITS

VERRINES

The trend for presenting desserts in glasses, called *verrines* in France, swept through the country's cooking magazines years ago, and it is still going strong. Verrines are usually around the 8-ounce size, but I have taken the liberty of making the following soft desserts in any sort of glass or small dish, including verrines. Think about using martini glasses, small bowls, parfait glasses, ramekins, or mini cocottes.

A CLOUD OF LEMON VERMOUTH MOUSSE

Une Mousse Légère au Vermouth et au Citron QUICKER | SERVES 6

This mousse is like dipping into a snowy-white cloud that disappears on your tongue. Its intriguing flavor comes from the combination of French vermouth and lemon and cream. It's one of the most asked-for recipes I make.

French vermouth is not as sweet as Italian vermouth, although it is made with sugar, white wine, herbs, and spices. If you can't find French vermouth, use Italian.

SPECIAL EQUIPMENT ELECTRIC STAND MIXER; 6 (8-OUNCE) VERRINES

3 large eggs, separated, room temperature

10 tablespoons dry white French vermouth, divided

3 organic lemons, 1 zested and 3 juiced

½ cup plus 5 tablespoons granulated sugar, divided

1 packet powdered gelatin

1 ½ cups whipping cream, chilled

In the bowl of the mixer, add 3 egg yolks, 6 tablespoons vermouth, lemon zest, ½ cup lemon juice, and ½ cup sugar and beat on medium until creamy, about 2 minutes.

Meanwhile, pour gelatin into a small bowl by the stove. Pour remaining vermouth into a small saucepan, bring to a boil, then pour over the gelatin in the bowl and stir until the crystals dissolve.

Slowly beat the dissolved gelatin into the egg mixture and continue beating on medium for 1 minute. Cover and place the bowl in the refrigerator so the mixture thickens and becomes like half-set gelatin.

At this point, beat the egg whites until they hold their shape, add 2 tablespoons sugar, continue to beat until the egg whites are stiff, then fold them into the refrigerated mixture.

Beat the cream with the remaining sugar until stiff, and then fold into the mixture, being careful to maintain volume and lightness.

Evenly divide the mousse between the glasses, cover with plastic wrap, and refrigerate for 3 hours or overnight. Serve with a thin butter cookie.

TRÈS QUICK CHOCOLATE GINGER POTS DE CRÈME

Pots de Crème Express au Chocolat et au Gingembre **QUICKER** | SERVES 6

Fast. Easy. Utterly delicious. All you do is whiz the ingredients together in a food processor and serve when it is chilled. Spoon a soft mound of whipped cream topped with chopped crystallized ginger onto the center of each.

SPECIAL EQUIPMENT FOOD PROCESSOR; 6 (8-OUNCE) GLASSES OR RAMEKINS

16 ounces best-quality semisweet chocolate, coarsely chopped

¼ teaspoon salt

1 ½ teaspoons ground ginger

¼ cup plus 1 tablespoon granulated sugar

2 ½ cups heavy whipping cream

3 large eggs, room temperature

2 ½ teaspoons pure vanilla extract

1 ⅓ cups coarsely chopped crystallized ginger, plus more for garnish

Sweetened whipped cream

Using the food processor, add the chocolate, salt, ground ginger, and sugar and process until finely ground.

Heat the whipping cream over medium heat and, when little bubbles form around the edges and it begins to come to a simmer, gradually pour it into the food processor with the machine running; process until the mixture is very smooth and blended.

Crack the eggs into the food processor. Add the vanilla and process for 10 seconds.

Stir in the chopped ginger then spoon into the glasses. Cool to room temperature, cover with plastic wrap, and refrigerate for 3 hours. Serve with a dollop of whipped cream.

TIP

You can also grate in some fresh ginger when you heat the milk for an added punch of flavor.

STRAWBERRIES ROMANOFF

Les Fraises Romanoff QUICKER | SERVES 4

The simplest of desserts, yet so iconic of classic French cuisine, strawberries Romanoff exemplifies the fact that sometimes a few good ingredients can come together to make a splendid dessert that everyone will enjoy.

It was created in the late 1800s by the famous chef Antonin Carême to present to the Russian Tsar Nicholas.

SPECIAL EQUIPMENT ELECTRIC HAND MIXER; 4 GLASS GOBLETS OR RAMEKINS

4 cups fresh strawberries, quartered, plus 4 whole berries for garnish

½ cup orange juice

3 tablespoons superfine sugar

¼ cup Curaçao liqueur (or Grand Marnier or Cointreau)

1 cup heavy whipping cream, chilled

3 tablespoons confectioner's sugar

1 teaspoon pure vanilla extract

Toss the berries together in a mixing bowl with the orange juice, superfine sugar, and Curaçao. Cover and refrigerate for 2 hours.

Using the mixer, whip the cream until soft peaks form. Sprinkle in the confectioner's sugar and beat until almost stiff peaks form. Beat in the vanilla.

Strain the strawberries and keep their juices. Divide the strawberries between the goblets, mound the whipped cream on top, and drizzle with the strawberry juices. Garnish with a whole berry.

TIP

You can also soften some vanilla ice cream, beat in the orange liqueur, fold in the whipped cream, divide between serving dishes, and top with the strawberries or a mix of other berries for a delicious variation. It would also be fun to serve this with chocolate-dipped fresh strawberries.

FRESH AND DRIED FRUIT SALAD IN SWEET BASIL SYRUP

Salade de Fruits Frais et Secs dans un Sirop au Basilic QUICKER | SERVES 6

Fruit desserts are popular in France, from sorbets to fruit-flavored ice cream to fruit with cheese to dainty glassfuls of fruit soup that appear at the side of a row of cookies in a chic restaurant. A fruit salad is one of the ways French families celebrate the bounty of summer.

When I was staying in a small auberge in the country, I was served a fresh fruit salad with a twist. They added dried fruits and pine nuts to it, and it was delicious. The recipe below is my rendition of that dish, to which I add a fresh basil sweet syrup. I present this on a large serving platter, or in a shallow bowl, and then fill individual glasses with it at the table. A final spoonful of basil syrup is ladled over the top with a couple of fresh basil leaves for garnish.

SPECIAL EQUIPMENT FOOD PROCESSOR; SERVING PLATTER OR LARGE SHALLOW BOWL; 6 (8-OUNCE) VERRINES

1 cup granulated sugar	1 cup pitted prunes, sliced in half	2 Granny Smith apples
1 cup water	1 teaspoon herbes de Provence	2 pears
1 cup tightly packed coarsely chopped basil, plus 12 leaves for garnish	2 bananas	¾ cup slivered almonds
	1 large navel orange	1 cup pomegranate seeds
2 cups dried apricots, sliced in half	½ lemon, juiced	

In a saucepan, heat the sugar and water until the sugar has dissolved and the mixture just starts to come to a simmer. Remove from the heat, add the basil, and set aside to infuse for 20 minutes. Pour into a food processor and process for 5 seconds. Strain through a fine mesh strainer into a large mixing bowl.

Place the apricots and prunes in a medium mixing bowl. Sprinkle with herbes de Provence then pour 2 cups boiling water over the top and allow to soften for 20 minutes. Using your hands, transfer the fruit to the large bowl and discard the soaking liquid. It is fine if there are still a few herbes de Provence in the fruit.

Slice the bananas into the large bowl and toss. Peel and slice the orange into large dice and add to the bowl. Toss to coat.

Have a bowl of water mixed with the lemon juice ready. Peel, core, and slice the apples into large dice, tossing them in the lemon water to keep them from browning. Repeat this process with the pears.

Strain the apples and pears and add them to the large bowl of fruit, tossing everything to coat really well. Add the almonds and toss again.

Spoon the fruit salad onto a serving platter, top with the pomegranate seeds, and bring to the table. Spoon into verrines at the table and top each with a leaf of basil.

TIP

This also works well with fresh mint leaves instead of basil, although any herb or edible flower would be an interesting addition.

GRAND MARNIER MOUSSE

Mousse au Grand Marnier QUICKER | SERVES 6

I firmly believe that adding Grand Marnier to almost anything makes it better. It's been made in France since 1880 with bitter oranges, sugar, and cognac and is an ingredient in many traditional French desserts.

Luxurious, thick, creamy, and with a kick from the orange zest, this wonderfully indulgent mousse is perfect for ending a dinner party.

SPECIAL EQUIPMENT 6 MARTINI GLASSES; ELECTRIC HAND MIXER

1 (3-ounce) semisweet chocolate bar, finely chopped

⅓ cup heavy cream

1 ½ cups half-and-half

2 tablespoons cornstarch

¼ cup plus 1 tablespoon granulated sugar

1 tablespoon honey

1 tablespoon unsalted butter

¼ cup plus 6 teaspoons Grand Marnier

1 tablespoon organic orange zest

1 cup heavy whipping cream

Place the chocolate into a heatproof bowl set over a saucepan of simmering water. Add the cream and melt the chocolate, stirring towards the end, until it is very smooth.

Dip a pastry brush or flat paint brush into the melted chocolate and decorate the serving glasses by painting a design on the inside of each glass. You can also dip a fork into the chocolate and wave it over the glasses for a random design. Place the glasses into the refrigerator for the chocolate to harden. Save any leftover chocolate.

Pour the half-and-half into a saucepan and whisk in the cornstarch until smooth. Add the sugar and

honey and bring to a boil. Reduce to a simmer and cook until the mixture thickens, whisking continuously, about 3 minutes. Add the butter and whisk until it melts. Allow to cool to room temperature for 15 minutes. Whisk in ¼ cup Grand Marnier and the orange zest.

Using the mixer, whip the cream until soft peaks form. Fold the whipped cream into the cooled mixture until well blended. Pour 1 teaspoon Grand Marnier into the bottom of each glass then evenly divide the mousse into each glass. Chill for 3 hours before serving.

SWEET WINE JELLY, WINE WHIPPED CREAM, AND GRAPES ON THE VINE

Gelée au Vin Doux, Chantilly au Vin, Petites Grappes de Raisins **LONGER** | SERVES 6

I make this with Muscat de Beaumes-de-Venise, the sweet dessert wine from the Rhône Valley in France, but any good sweet dessert wine works. You can also easily substitute red or rosé for the white wine. If you do, taste as you go because you will need to add more sugar. During the holidays, try flavoring it with mulled wine spices.

SPECIAL EQUIPMENT 6 (8-OUNCE) VERRINES; ELECTRIC HAND MIXER

6 cups plus 7 tablespoons sweet
    dessert wine, divided

2 tablespoons granulated sugar

3 ¾ packets powdered gelatin

1 ½ cups whipping cream, chilled

3 tablespoons confectioner's
    sugar

¼ teaspoon pure vanilla extract

6 small branches seedless red or
    green grapes on the vine, plus
    12 individual grapes

Bring 5 cups plus 6 tablespoons wine and the granulated sugar to a boil.

Pour 1 cup of the remaining wine into a large shallow bowl and sprinkle all of the gelatin over the top, mixing once with a fork so it is all coated. Leave the gelatin to absorb the liquid for 2 minutes.

Add the dissolved gelatin to the boiling wine and whisk; cook for 1 minute, until the gelatin is melted. Pour into a large heatproof bowl for the mixture to cool down enough to pour into the glasses. Then divide between the glasses. Cover and refrigerate for 3 hours until firm.

Whip the cream until soft peaks form. Add confectioner's sugar, vanilla, and remaining 1 tablespoon wine and beat again until the cream regains shape and is mounding in soft peaks.

Place 2 grapes on the center of each jelly. Spoon the whipped cream in gentle mounds over the top of the grapes to hide them and either hang a branch of fresh grapes on the rim of each glass or serve them on the side on a plate.

TIP

You can chill the jelly in one large shaped mold instead of the individual verrines. If you do, pour a little vegetable oil on a paper towel and lightly grease the interior to make it easy for the jelly to slip out.

LEMON RICE PUDDING WITH BLACKBERRY CARAMEL SAUCE

Riz au Lait au citron, Sauce Caramel aux Mûres LONGER | SERVES 6

I adore almost any kind of rice pudding. This one is cooked on the stovetop, is thick and rich, and has overtones of honey and lemon. Serve it warm or chilled with blackberry caramel sauce floating on top.

SPECIAL EQUIPMENT: 6 (8-OUNCE) VERRINES OR RAMEKINS; FOOD PROCESSOR

Pudding

¾ cup Arborio rice

¼ teaspoon salt

¼ cup granulated sugar

4 cups half-and-half

2 large egg yolks, room temperature

2 tablespoons unsalted butter, softened

½ cup honey

1 teaspoon lemon extract

½ teaspoon pure vanilla extract

1 medium organic lemon, zested then juiced

Blackberry Caramel Sauce

1 cup light brown sugar

½ cup half-and-half

1 tablespoon unsalted butter

¾ cup fresh or frozen and thawed blackberries

Zest of ½ organic lemon

12 fresh blackberries

PUDDING

In a saucepan, add the rice, salt, sugar, and half-and-half. Bring to a boil, carefully watching so that it does not boil over. When it is just about at a boil, immediately reduce to a gentle slow simmer, whisking now and again.

Cook, and occasionally whisk, until the rice is very tender, the mixture is thick, and most of the liquid has been absorbed. I vigorously whisk, rather than stir, my rice pudding to break up the rice a bit and release starch for a thicker, creamier texture. This process takes about 30 minutes.

Beat the egg yolks with a whisk for about 30 seconds. Spoon in some of the hot rice mixture and whisk to warm up the eggs before scooping them into the hot rice and vigorously whisking.

Remove from the heat and continue whisking for about 30 seconds. Whisk in the butter until it is melted and blended in. Now vigorously whisk in the honey until well blended. Pour in the lemon extract, vanilla extract, and lemon juice and add the lemon zest then whisk to combine.

Divide between the glasses or ramekins, cover, and refrigerate until ready to serve.

BLACKBERRY CARAMEL SAUCE

Add the brown sugar, half-and-half, butter, ¾ cup blackberries, and lemon zest to the food processor and process until smooth. Scoop into a saucepan and cook over medium heat while whisking for 4 minutes. Cool to room temperature then refrigerate for 15 minutes.

To serve, remove the rice puddings from the refrigerator 15 minutes before serving, evenly divide the blackberry sauce over the top, add 2 blackberries to the center of each, and serve.

PROVENÇAL MELON MOUSSE

Mousse Provençale au Melon LONGER | SERVES 6

There are small petal-shaped cookies made in Provence called calissons, *which date from the fifteenth century and are a specialty of Aix-en-Provence. They are partially a cookie, partially a candy, and made from candied melons, candied oranges, and ground almonds. I took inspiration from calissons to create this recipe for a melon mousse.*

In my interpretation, a richly textured almond mousse is made with almond paste then mixed with a purée of fresh canta-loupe. It's a light and refreshing mousse with a decidedly Provençal accent.

SPECIAL EQUIPMENT FOOD PROCESSOR; ELECTRIC HAND MIXER; 6 (8-OUNCE) VERRINES OR RAMEKINS

2 tablespoons cornstarch

⅓ cup plus 1 tablespoon granulated sugar, divided

1 tablespoon warm water

1 ½ teaspoons unflavored gelatin

2 large eggs, room temperature

2 large egg yolks, room temperature

7 ounces almond paste

1 cup almond milk

1 teaspoon almond extract

3 cups cubed cantaloupe plus 6 (½-inch-thick) wedges

1 cup heavy whipping cream, chilled

Whisk together the cornstarch and ⅓ cup sugar in a small bowl then toss into the food processor.

Pour the water into a small bowl. Sprinkle the gelatin over the water and leave to dissolve for 5 minutes.

Add the eggs and egg yolks to the food processor. Crumble in the almond paste. Pour in the almond milk and process until smooth. Pour this mixture into a saucepan and bring to a boil, constantly whisking. Once it reaches a boil, remove from the heat. Pour 2 tablespoons of this hot mixture into the gelatin and mix well then add the gelatin mixture to the saucepan, place back on the heat, and whisk on medium heat for 2 minutes. Whisk in the almond extract.

Remove from the heat, pour into a large heat-proof bowl, cool to room temperature, then cover and place in the refrigerator for 20 minutes to chill.

In the meantime, toss the cubed melon and remaining sugar into the food processor and pulse until the melon is broken down into tiny pieces. Take the almond custard out of the refrigerator and whisk all of the melon mixture into it, including any juice.

Whip the cream until peaks form. Fold in a third of the almond custard then fold in the rest until just blended. Evenly divide between the glasses or ramekins and refrigerate for 3 hours.

To serve, place a glass or ramekin on a dessert plate and lean a wedge of melon against it.

CHAMBORD RASPBERRY AND WHITE CHOCOLATE MOUSSE

Mousse Chambord aux Framboises et au Chocolat Blanc **LONGER** | SERVES 6

Raspberries and white chocolate are a great combination. This recipe features the raspberry liqueur Chambord, produced in the Loire Valley of France. It is made from red and black raspberries, vanilla, honey, and cognac. Combined with white chocolate and accented with fresh berries, it is divine in this simple mousse.

SPECIAL EQUIPMENT ELECTRIC HAND MIXER; 6 (8-OUNCE) VERRINES

4 large egg yolks, room temperature

5 tablespoons granulated sugar, divided

¼ cup Chambord, plus more for drizzling

1 pint raspberries, plus 12 whole berries

4 ounces white chocolate, broken into pieces

1 cup whipping cream, chilled

1 teaspoon pure vanilla extract

6 mint leaves, optional

In a heatproof bowl, add the egg yolks, 2 tablespoons sugar, and ¼ cup Chambord and whisk to combine.

Place the bowl over a pan of simmering water and vigorously whisk while cooking until the egg mixture thickens and coats the back of a spoon, 1–2 minutes. It will look thick and foamy. Whisk in the pint of raspberries, crushing with the whisk until well combined. Cool the mixture to room temperature.

Melt the white chocolate in a microwave, stir until creamy, then scoop into the egg mixture and whisk well to combine.

Whip the cream until soft peaks form, add remaining sugar and the vanilla and beat again until stiff peaks form. Fold the whipped cream into the egg mixture then divide between glasses and refrigerate for 5 hours.

Serve with a small liqueur glass of Chambord to the side if you wish. If you have mint leaves, place one on the top of each mousse along with a couple of raspberries.

BLANC-MANGER WITH APRICOT COULIS

Blanc-Manger et Coulis d'Abricot **LONGER** | MAKES 4 VERRINES

Blanc-manger *is a refreshing, creamy almond-flavored French dessert that dates from the Middle Ages when it began as a savory dish. It's usually made from almonds, milk, sugar, and gelatin.*

For a simple, light dessert tasting of almonds and apricots, I've added an apricot coulis to mine, with the blanc-manger on top. Garnish with a sprig of mint dusted with confectioner's sugar.

SPECIAL EQUIPMENT FOOD PROCESSOR; 4 (8-OUNCE) VERRINES; ELECTRIC HAND MIXER

Blanc-manger

½ cup slivered almonds

¾ cup almond milk

½ cup plus 2 tablespoons granulated sugar

2 teaspoons powdered gelatin

1 ½ teaspoons pure almond extract

½ teaspoon pure vanilla extract

1 ½ cups whipping cream, chilled

Sliced almonds, optional

Apricot Coulis

1 cup dried apricots

1 cup orange juice or water, divided

4 tablespoons granulated sugar

BLANC-MANGER

Grind the almonds in the food processor until finely ground.

In a saucepan, bring the almond milk, ground almonds, and sugar to a boil, whisking so that the sugar dissolves.

Pour the gelatin into a small bowl by the stove. Heat 4 tablespoons water in a small saucepan and when it comes to a boil, pour it over the gelatin and stir until the gelatin is dissolved.

Slowly beat the gelatin with a whisk into the hot almond milk; continue to whisk and cook for 30 seconds then remove from the heat. Whisk in the almond and vanilla extracts. Pour into a heatproof bowl, let cool to room temperature, then refrigerate for 20 minutes.

APRICOT COULIS

Meanwhile, make the apricot coulis. In a saucepan, heat the apricots, ½ cup orange juice, and sugar. Bring to a gentle boil and let it cook for 2 minutes. Pour this into the food processor and process until smooth. Pour in remaining orange juice and process until smooth. Divide the apricot mixture into the bottom of each serving glass.

Whip the cream until stiff. Gently fold the whipped cream into the refrigerated almond milk mixture and divide evenly between the glasses. Refrigerate for at least 1 hour before serving. Garnish with sliced almonds.

FROZEN OR REFRIGERATED DESSERTS

To keep cool in the summer, I pull out my ice cream machine and use it frequently to take advantage of ripe summer fruit. When I lived in the village of Bar-sur-Loup, known as the "village of oranges" because of all the orange trees in the area, I had a steady supply of oranges as well as other local fruit to work with. Making frozen or refrigerated desserts in the summer also means no baking on a hot day. The following are my best-of-show chilly French desserts.

"VIN CHAUD" SORBET WITH FROSTED GRAPES

Sorbet au "Vin Chaud" et Raisins Givrés QUICKER | MAKES 1 QUART

In Alsace, in the French Alps, and in cafés in Paris during the winter, vin chaud, *hot-spiced wine, is sipped to warm up and slow down after a cold walk or a day of skiing. I love the flavor so much that I also freeze mine into a sorbet to enjoy in the summer. This dessert is child friendly because you cook off the alcohol so that the wine will freeze.*

SPECIAL EQUIPMENT ICE CREAM MACHINE; PARCHMENT PAPER; 1 BAKING SHEET

Sorbet

½ cup plus 2 tablespoons granulated sugar

¾ cup water

1 tablespoon light corn syrup

1 bottle full-bodied red wine (Beaujolais, Merlot, or Pinot Noir)

2 star anise

1 cinnamon stick, broken in half

3 whole cloves

1 strip orange rind

Frosted Grapes

2 bunches green or red grapes, washed and dried

2 large egg whites beaten with 2 teaspoons water

¾ cup granulated sugar

SORBET

Add the sugar, water, corn syrup, wine, star anise, cinnamon stick, cloves, and orange rind to a saucepan and bring to a vigorous boil then boil for 3 minutes, until the alcohol is cooked off. Turn off the heat and allow to steep for 5 minutes.

Strain through a fine mesh sieve into a bowl and allow to cool to room temperature. Cover with plastic wrap and place in the refrigerator until well chilled. To speed up the process, place the bowl over another bowl of ice and stir until cool before placing in the refrigerator.

Process the sorbet in the ice cream machine according to manufacturer's instructions.

FROSTED GRAPES

Use a pastry brush to paint the grapes with the egg wash so they are entirely wet and coated.

Lay down a piece of parchment paper on the baking sheet and place the bunches of grapes on it. Liberally sprinkle the grapes with the sugar to coat then turn over and repeat on the other side. Place the baking sheet in the freezer until you are ready to serve the sorbet.

Scoop the sorbet into beautiful glasses or small bowls and garnish with the frozen grapes.

TIP

Scoop out balls of the sorbet onto a piece of parchment paper in the freezer and keep them there until ready to assemble your dessert in the glasses or bowls. An ice cream scoop with a spring loaded sweeper makes scooping perfect balls much easier.

The "Vin Chaud" Sorbet is the darker-colored frozen treat in this photo. The pink scoops are Strawberry Frozen Yogurt. See recipe on (page 124).

STRAWBERRY FROZEN YOGURT

Yaourt Glacé aux Fraises QUICKER | MAKES 1 QUART

I was waiting for lunch but thinking about dessert. I was at a restaurant in Nice, thinking about the dessert I had seen on the menu. Should I order it? It was called Balsamic Ice Cream. Yes, I decided. I definitely would try it. It came with fresh strawberry slices. I can still remember the pleasure from tasting the combination. I built on that memory and created this recipe where it all comes together within the ice cream, the sweet strawberries and the tang of yogurt and balsamic vinegar. It's a luscious, creamy dessert that will surprise and delight you, as it did me.

SPECIAL EQUIPMENT FOOD PROCESSOR; ICE CREAM MACHINE

2 ½ cups fresh strawberries, coarsely chopped

2 cups vanilla Greek yogurt

1 teaspoon pure vanilla extract

½ cup plus 3 tablespoons granulated sugar

2 teaspoons balsamic vinegar

1 tablespoon vodka

Add everything except the vodka to the food processor and process until smooth. Transfer to a bowl, cover, and place in the freezer until very well chilled. Stir in the vodka, pour into the ice cream machine, and process according to manufacturer's instructions.

TIP

Don't leave out the vodka; it helps prevent iciness in the frozen yogurt.

See the previous page for a photograph of this recipe.

PEACH MELBA WITH MUDDLED VANILLA ICE CREAM

Pêche Melba, Glace à la Vanille Marbrée de Purée de Framboises Fraîches

QUICKER | SERVES 4

I teach this dessert in my retro French cooking classes. Invented by the great French chef Auguste Escoffier in 1892, Peach Melba was created in honor of the opera star, Nellie Melba. It is most often presented in a wide, shallow champagne glass with peaches under a purée of raspberries and a ring of whipped cream with fresh raspberries around them.

SPECIAL EQUIPMENT FOOD PROCESSOR; ELECTRIC HAND MIXER

Peaches

4 large ripe peaches

3 cups water

2 cups granulated sugar

1 tablespoon pure vanilla extract

½ lemon, juiced

Raspberry Purée

1 (10-ounce) package frozen raspberries, thawed and drained

3 tablespoons confectioner's sugar

Whipped Cream

1 cup heavy whipping cream, chilled

3 tablespoons superfine sugar

2 teaspoons pure vanilla extract

To serve

1 pint vanilla ice cream, softened

16 fresh raspberries for garnish

PEACHES

Pour cold water into a bowl and add some ice cubes.

Blanch the peaches in boiling water for 3–4 seconds. With a slotted spoon, transfer them to the ice water. When they are cool to the touch, peel them with a small paring knife. Slice them in half and discard the pits.

In a saucepan large enough to hold all the peaches, bring the water and sugar to a boil and stir until the sugar dissolves. Turn down the heat to low and place the peaches in the hot syrup, being careful not to splash on your skin. Simmer until the peaches just turn fork tender, 8–10 minutes. Remove from the heat and stir in the vanilla and lemon juice. Put everything into a large bowl, including the syrup, cover, and refrigerate until the peaches are very cold.

RASPBERRY PURÉE

Purée the raspberries and sugar in the food processor until very smooth. Refrigerate.

WHIPPED CREAM

Using the mixer, beat the cream until soft peaks form. Add the sugar and vanilla and beat again until soft peaks form. Refrigerate.

TO SERVE

When you are ready to serve the peaches, scoop all of the ice cream into a mixing bowl and muddle or mash it down with a spoon until it loses shape. Divide this between each serving glass or bowl.

Add 2 peach halves to each glass and discard the peach syrup. Divide the raspberry purée evenly over the top. Dollop the whipped cream in a circle around the peaches and garnish with raspberries.

TIP

You can add 2 tablespoons Chambord raspberry liqueur to the purée to enhance it, if you like.

FRESH ORANGE SORBET CHAMPAGNE COUPE

Coupe Glacée de Sorbet à l'Orange Fraîche et Champagne **QUICKER** | SERVES 6

Better than a mimosa, this chilly dessert is a revelation because making your own orange sorbet for it tremendously boosts the flavor. I first had it in one of the grand hotels along the sea in Cannes. It came in a tall crystal champagne glass placed on a paper doily set on a large plate with paper-thin tuiles to the side. It made such an impression on me that I went home, made my own orange sorbet, and served it this way on the weekend for a celebration with friends—who also loved it.

SPECIAL EQUIPMENT FOOD PROCESSOR; ICE CREAM MACHINE; 6 TALL WINE OR PARFAIT GLASSES

1 teaspoon finely grated organic
  orange zest

¾ cup granulated sugar

2 ¾ cups freshly squeezed
  organic orange juice

¼ cup freshly squeezed lemon
  juice

2 star anise

3 cups champagne or sparkling
  wine, or more for larger glasses

Add the orange zest to the food processor with the sugar and process for 10 seconds so that the orange oil flavors the sugar. Pour the orange-scented sugar into a saucepan.

Place the orange juice, lemon juice, and star anise in the saucepan with the sugar and whisk while cooking on medium heat until you bring the mixture to a boil. Boil for 30 seconds. Take off the heat, pour into a heatproof bowl, cool to room temperature, then put in the refrigerator until it is very cold.

Discard the star anise then process the mixture in the ice cream maker according to manufacturer's instructions. Scoop into a container, cover, and freeze.

To serve, add a scoop or two of the sorbet to each glass and divide the champagne over the top of each.

TIP

You can use this recipe for orange sorbet to make the other French classic, Orange Givrée. Cut the top off an orange, remove the inside flesh and replace it with orange sorbet, then freeze until ready to serve.

LEFT BANK CAFÉ LIÉGEOIS

Café Liégeois "Rive Gauche" **QUICKER** | SERVES 4

Another classic French dessert, café liégeois was renamed from the original café viennois to honor the Belgian city of Liège for its resistance to the Germans during World War I. It's one of those desserts you have once, on a hot summer day, and never forget—especially if you are a coffee lover. Pour ice-cold coffee or espresso into a glass, add coffee ice cream, and top it with whipped cream. I often add a little espresso to the whipped cream as well.

SPECIAL EQUIPMENT ELECTRIC STAND MIXER; ICE CREAM MACHINE; 4 GLASSES OR DESSERT BOWLS

3 cups half-and-half

¼ cup light brown sugar

2 tablespoons instant espresso powder

1 teaspoon ground cinnamon

1 ½ teaspoons pure vanilla extract, divided

5 egg yolks

½ cup granulated sugar

1 cup whipping cream, chilled

3 tablespoons confectioner's sugar

2 cups brewed coffee or espresso, chilled and sweetened

In a saucepan, add the half-and-half, brown sugar, and the espresso powder. Whisk while bringing to a simmer and cook until the sugar is melted and blended. Take off the heat and whisk in the cinnamon and ½ teaspoon vanilla.

Using the mixer, beat the egg yolks with the granulated sugar until pale and fluffy, about 5 minutes. Slowly pour in the half-and-half mixture while beating on low.

Pour everything back into the saucepan and, over medium heat, whisk while cooking until the mixture thickens, about 5 minutes. Pour into a heat-proof bowl, cool to room temperature, cover with plastic wrap, and refrigerate until very cold.

Process the mixture in the ice cream machine according to manufacturer's instructions.

Before serving, beat the cream until soft peaks form. Add the confectioner's sugar and remaining vanilla and beat until almost stiff peak stage.

To serve, add scoops of ice cream to chilled glasses. Pour coffee into each glass and top with whipped cream.

TIPS

Use a vegetable peeler to scrape along the edge of a chilled bar of chocolate to make chocolate curls for the top, if you would like. This dessert is also nice garnished with chocolate-covered almonds, chocolate-covered espresso beans, or rainbow-colored sprinkles. You can also add 1 tablespoon of coffee liqueur to the cold coffee.

PEACH SORBET WITH FRESH PEACH SLICES

Sorbet à la Pêche, Tranches de Pêches Fraîches **QUICKER** | SERVES 6 TO 8

A friend brought me four huge misshapen ripe peaches from her tree, and when I used them to make a sorbet, I was convinced to spend more time making sorbets with fresh fruit. It intensifies the flavor and refreshes at the same time, offering a light alternative after a heavy meal.

SPECIAL EQUIPMENT FOOD PROCESSOR; ICE CREAM MACHINE

4 large ripe peaches, plus 3 for garnish

1 tablespoon vodka

1 cup granulated sugar

1 lime, juiced

No need to peel the 4 peaches. Just wash and dry them, slice them, and discard the pits. Toss the peach slices into the food processor with the vodka, sugar, and lime juice. Purée until very smooth.

Pour this mixture into your ice cream maker and follow the manufacturer's instructions. Transfer to a freezer container and freeze until ready to serve.

When ready to serve, take the sorbet out of the freezer and allow to stand for 10 minutes to soften.

Wash and dry 3 peaches and slice them. Scoop the peach sorbet into glasses or bowls and garnish with fresh peach slices.

VANILLA, RASPBERRY, AND CHOCOLATE ICE CREAM BOMBE GLACÉE

Bombe Glacée Vanille, Framboise et Chocolat **LONGER** | SERVES 8

An ice cream bombe is French retro. Rarely found in restaurants anymore, it is fun to prepare at home. It takes a while because it is done in stages, so plan to make it one day and serve it the next.

You first freeze a layer of ice cream or sorbet in a bowl, then add another layer and freeze, then add the next, with each layer taking 1–2 hours to harden in the freezer. Make the dark chocolate sauce to pour over the top and, if you wish, decorate more elaborately with rosettes of whipped cream, shavings of chocolate, and a cherry crowning the top.

SPECIAL EQUIPMENT 1 (8-INCH) METAL BOWL

Bombe	Sauce
2 pints vanilla ice cream	8 ounces semisweet chocolate
1 ½ pints raspberry sorbet	3 tablespoons butter
1 pint chocolate ice cream	1 teaspoon pure vanilla extract

BOMBE

Freeze the bowl then line it with plastic wrap that extends 4 inches all the way around.

Thaw the vanilla ice cream until it is soft enough to work with, spoon it into the plastic wrap–lined bowl, wet a spoon, and push the ice cream to the sides and bottom of the bowl in a thick, even layer, bringing it all the way up to the rim.

Lay a piece of plastic wrap over the vanilla ice cream and use your fingers to press down and smooth out this layer. Place in the freezer so that the layer hardens a little, about 35 minutes, and then use the back of a large spoon to smooth the layer and put it in the freezer again for 2 hours.

Thaw the raspberry sorbet so that it is softened when the bowl comes out of the freezer.

Take the bowl out of the freezer and remove the plastic wrap. Spread the raspberry sorbet over the frozen vanilla layer in a concave bowl shape,

bringing it up all the way to the rim. Put a layer of plastic wrap over it and use your fingers to smooth the raspberry sorbet into a concave shape that will hold the final layer of chocolate ice cream. Then use a large spoon to smooth again. Freeze for 1 ½ hours.

Repeat the process with the final layer of chocolate ice cream, finally covering the bowl with plastic wrap and freezing for 4 hours or overnight.

When you are ready to serve it, place a serving plate on top, invert, and take off the plastic wrap. At this point you can freeze it until you are ready for it, or serve it right away.

SAUCE

To make the sauce, place all the ingredients into a saucepan and melt. Allow to cool to room temperature.

When ready, pour the chocolate sauce over the bombe, run a knife under hot water, slice into 8 pieces, and serve.

BOULANGER
PATISSIER

MAISON LACORNE
pain de tradition

WAFFLES, CRÊPES, AND PANCAKES

During the Christian holiday called *Chandeleur* (Candlemas), which falls on the second day of February every year, the French celebrate by making crêpes. After eight p.m. on that day, they cook them to wish for a good and prosperous year ahead and for good crops for the farmers. Throughout the year, crêpes are celebrated in *crêperies* throughout France where they are made in both savory and sweet varieties. In this chapter I have included a recipe for a classic Crêpes Suzette, still one of my favorite ways to have crêpes.

Gaufres, or waffles, are cooked fresh at street stalls and fairs and are hard to pass up when you walk by and see them garnished with salted caramel or chocolate or whipped cream and berries. It's a great walk-around snack that you already know how to make at home.

I've also included a recipe for a sweet *matefaim*, which means "suppress or tame the appetite." Matefaims originate from the area around Lyon and are thick pancakes typically made with potatoes or apples.

STREET FAIR LEMON WAFFLES WITH BLUEBERRIES AND CHANTILLY

Gaufres au Citron Comme à la Foire, Myrtilles et Crème Chantilly

QUICKER | MAKES 8 TO 10 WAFFLES

On a cold, snowy day in Paris, I tasted my first hot waffle covered in powdered sugar. I bought it from a street stand and stood there devouring every last morsel, in love with the warmth, the crunch, the melting confectioner's sugar, and the snow flakes melting at the same time on my cheeks.

Waffles have been sold in the streets of France as a snack for centuries, especially on festive occasions like fairs or festivals. I buy one every chance I get, hoping for the same experience I had that snowy day in Paris. If not, I make them at home, jazzed up a bit. Mine are lemony waffles served with whipped cream and blueberries. I also like to serve them with a sprinkling of lemon sugar. I zest an organic lemon and whiz it in the food processor with 1 cup sugar so the lemon oil permeates the sugar and, sprinkled over the top, adds another dimension to the lemon waffles.

SPECIAL EQUIPMENT CITRUS MICROPLANE; ELECTRIC HAND MIXER; WAFFLE IRON; 1 BAKING SHEET

Cooking spray for waffle iron

2 organic lemons

2 large eggs, room temperature, separated

1 cup half-and-half

½ cup plus 3 tablespoons granulated sugar

1 teaspoon pure vanilla extract

1 teaspoon lemon extract

1 cup cake flour

1 cup all-purpose flour

2 ½ teaspoons baking powder

½ teaspoon salt

1 stick butter, melted

2 cups fresh blueberries

Sweetened whipped cream

Preheat oven to 250 degrees F if you plan to keep the waffles warm until serving. Preheat the waffle iron and spray with cooking spray.

Use the microplane to zest the lemons then divide the zest into 2 piles. Juice the lemons to measure ½ cup lemon juice.

In a large mixing bowl, whisk together 2 egg yolks, half-and-half, the lemon juice, sugar, vanilla and lemon extracts, and 1 pile of the lemon zest.

Sift the cake and all-purpose flours, baking powder, and salt into the egg yolk mixture. Whisk just until combined. Whisk in the butter.

Using the mixer, beat the 2 egg whites until they are stiff. Fold, do not stir, the egg whites into the batter until combined. They will make the waffles crisp and light.

Following the manufacturer's instructions, scoop some of the batter onto the center of the hot waffle iron and make a waffle. Repeat using the remaining batter. Transfer the waffles to a warm baking sheet in the heated oven until all the waffles are done.

To serve, mound whipped cream on top, scatter with blueberries, and garnish with the remaining pile of lemon zest.

FARZ BUEN BROKEN CRÊPES

Le Farz Buen QUICKER | SERVES 4

This is a family recipe from my friends in Brittany. I saw them make it for their children when I was visiting them, and I swooned. I'd never seen anything like it, I'd never heard about it, and I was totally smitten.

You make it in a frying pan with a crêpe batter that cooks as you add in butter and sugar. Then you take your spatula and break the crêpe up into little pieces, as you would when you make scrambled eggs. The little pieces become soft golden pillows that caramelize and are utterly irresistible. Top with a bit more butter and sugar then serve.

SPECIAL EQUIPMENT 1 LARGE NONSTICK FRYING PAN

¼ cup plus 3 tablespoons granulated sugar, divided

2 large eggs

2 cups plus 2 tablespoons all-purpose flour

1 ¾ cups half-and-half

2 tablespoons salted butter, divided

Preheat oven to 250 degrees F. In a mixing bowl, whisk together ¼ cup plus 2 tablespoons sugar and the eggs. Sift in half the flour, add half the half-and-half, and whisk vigorously to combine. Add the rest of the flour and half-and-half and whisk to combine.

Heat the frying pan then add 1 tablespoon butter. Pour in the batter to coat the bottom of the pan and let it set until it looks like the bottom is cooked. Begin to break it all up, slicing it with a fork and knife as it cooks, until it looks like scrambled eggs.

Add remaining butter, sprinkle with remaining sugar, and, as the mixture cooks, move it around and break it up more. Cook until it is lightly browned and caramelized.

If you have any remaining batter, place the farz buen in the oven to keep warm while you repeat the process, adding more batter and sugar as needed.

Spoon it all into a big bowl and serve with a spoon. I serve it as it is, but you can also serve it with a drizzle of melted jam or a drizzle of melted ice cream.

GREEN AND RED APPLE PANCAKE

Matefaim aux Pommes Vertes et Rouges **QUICKER** | SERVES 4

Matefaims, or matafans, from the Franche-Comté region in eastern France that borders Switzerland, means "calming or taming hunger." Most often they are thick, savory pancakes made with mashed potato. I was hiking with friends there and they packed potato matefaims made into sandwiches with ham and cheese for our portable lunch. They told me they also like to make them when they come back from a day of skiing or in a sweet version with apples for an afternoon snack.

My recipe has apples, both red and green, and I often add a dash of cognac to the batter.

SPECIAL EQUIPMENT 1 LARGE NONSTICK FRYING PAN

1 ½ cups all-purpose flour

1 tablespoon baking soda

¼ teaspoon salt

¼ cup plus 4 tablespoons granulated sugar, divided

2 large eggs, room temperature

3 tablespoons vegetable oil

3 teaspoons pure vanilla extract

1 cup milk

2 red apples

3 Granny Smith apples

2 tablespoons unsalted butter

Confectioner's sugar

Grated chocolate, optional

In a large mixing bowl, whisk the flour, baking soda, salt, and ¼ cup plus 2 tablespoons granulated sugar to combine.

In another bowl, whisk the eggs, oil, and vanilla extract together. Pour the wet ingredients into the dry ingredients, mix with a wooden spoon until smooth and all lumps disappear, then gradually whisk in the milk.

Let the mixture rest while you prepare the apples.

Slice 1 red and 2 green apples into 4 sections each. Peel, core, and slice each section very thinly. Slice these pieces in half. Melt butter in the pan with 1 tablespoon granulated sugar. Add the apples and cook them on medium heat until tender, about

4 minutes. Sprinkle in the remaining sugar and cook until the apples are caramelized and browned, 2–3 minutes.

Add the apples to the pancake batter and stir to combine. Scoop all of the batter into the pan and cook over medium-low heat without moving for about 15–20 minutes. Place a plate over the top, invert, and slide the pancake back into the pan to cook for another 4 minutes.

Garnish with the remaining apples that you have sliced into slivers, leaving the skin on for color, then sift confectioner's sugar over the top. Garnish with the chocolate, if you wish.

FRESH ORANGE CRÊPES SUZETTE

Crêpes Suzette à l'Orange Fraîche QUICKER | MAKES 16 (7-INCH) CRÊPES

My first introduction to crêpes was to be served Crêpes Suzette. I was eight years old and it was my father's favorite way of cooking a treat for us. He would bring out the crêpe pan he bought in Paris, make the crêpes in the kitchen, then prepare an orange Grand Marnier sauce at the table while we watched. We'd witness his careful folding of each crêpe, lowering them into the bubbling sauce and tenderly spooning the sauce over each one. Finally he would light it on fire. That was a huge hit. I still have his crêpe pan and his recipe, which follows.

I love the history of the dish. It was an accident, allegedly invented when a waiter was serving crêpes to the Prince of Wales and mistakenly set the sauce on fire. The sauce is not set on fire in this recipe in order to keep the punch of the Grand Marnier intact.

SPECIAL EQUIPMENT ELECTRIC BLENDER; 1 CRÊPE PAN OR NONSTICK SKILLET; PARCHMENT PAPER

Crêpes

1 cup milk

½ cup plus 3 tablespoons organic orange juice

1 teaspoon pure vanilla extract

5 tablespoons granulated sugar

½ teaspoon salt

3 large eggs, room temperature

1 ½ cups all-purpose flour

4 tablespoons unsalted butter, melted, plus butter for cooking the crêpes

Sauce

4 organic oranges, 1 zested

2 cups organic orange juice

¼ cup granulated sugar

¼ cup Grand Marnier, or any orange liqueur

1 teaspoon pure vanilla extract

CRÊPES

Add the milk, orange juice, vanilla, sugar, salt, and eggs to the blender and blend. Add the flour all at once and blend. Add the melted butter and blend. Let the batter rest for 30 minutes in the blender then blend once again before using.

Preheat oven to 250 degrees F.

Begin to cook your crêpes by putting a small amount of butter in the pan and cooking it until it melts and begins to sizzle.

Pour a ladle of batter in the pan and let it sit for 3 seconds then tip the pan into the blender, twirling the pan as you do, so you are left with a very thin layer of batter to cook in the bottom of the pan and any excess pours back into the blender.

Cook the crêpes on medium low and have patience. They need to cook through without burning and remain tender in the middle, with a slight crispness around the edges. Err on the side of cooking them slowly. As you cook them, put a piece of parchment paper between them and keep them in the warm oven.

SAUCE

Peel the oranges and slice from the ends into thin circles and reserve.

Pour the orange juice and sugar into a saucepan and bring to a boil, reduce to a simmer, and cook for 4 minutes. Remove from the heat and whisk in the Grand Marnier, vanilla, and orange zest. Toss in all of the orange slices and gently stir to coat. Keep warm.

To serve, divide the crêpes between 4 plates, folding them into quarters or rolling them into logs. Using a fork, pick up the orange slices and divide them over the crêpes then pour the sauce over the top and serve.

TIP

These are really pretty made with blood oranges or Cara Cara oranges.

PUFF PASTRY

Puff pastry, *pâte feuilletée*, is considered to be one of the hardest of all pastries to make. Someday I will try. Until then, I use all-butter ready-made frozen puff pastry from the market. It means I can create fast, fun desserts in minutes. Most families in France do exactly the same thing.

NIFLETTES

Les Niflettes de Provins QUICKER | MAKES 12 TO 16 (3-INCH) PASTRIES

These small pastries are a specialty of Provins, where folklore says they were created either by a baker or by women of the village to console orphans crying over the loss of their parents or grandparents. Niflette allegedly comes from the Latin "ne flette," which means "do not cry." They have become the traditional pastry offered in Provins on All Saints Day, when families visit the cemetery to commemorate their dead relatives.

Although initially a sad thought, I think the act of making them to soothe and bring happiness is reason enough to replicate them at home, don't you? How could sweet puff pastry and vanilla pastry cream not be comforting?

SPECIAL EQUIPMENT ROLLING PIN; 3-INCH DIAMETER COOKIE CUTTER OR GLASS; 2 BAKING SHEETS LINED WITH PARCHMENT PAPER

2 packages store-bought frozen puff pastry (4 sheets)

2 large egg yolks

¼ cup plus 2 teaspoons granulated sugar

⅛ teaspoon salt

1 tablespoon all-purpose flour

1 cup milk

1 teaspoon pure vanilla extract

1 egg beaten with 1 teaspoon water

Turbinado or granulated sugar

Thaw pastry according to package instructions. Preheat oven to 350 degrees F.

In a large bowl, whisk the egg yolks, sugar, and salt until thick and pale. Sprinkle the flour over the top and whisk well to blend.

In a saucepan, heat the milk until bubbles begin to appear around the edges. Gradually pour a thin stream of milk into the egg mixture while whisking until it is well combined with the eggs. Pour everything back into the saucepan and cook over medium heat while stirring with a wooden spoon until it becomes a thick pudding consistency. Whisk in the vanilla and leave to cool to room temperature.

Meanwhile, roll out the pastry sheets to 10 x 11-inch rectangles. Use cookie cutter to cut out rounds from the pastry sheets.

Place 1 round on the baking sheet, brush with the egg wash, place another round on top, and use your fingers to gently press in the center to make an indent where the vanilla pastry cream will be poured. Prick the center a couple of times with a fork. Brush the top round with the egg wash, including the outer edges. Sprinkle the outer edges with the turbinado sugar to make a crunchy rim. Repeat this process with the remaining pastry rounds.

Spoon the pastry cream into the hollow center of each round and bake for 20–25 minutes, until golden. Remove from the oven, use a spatula to remove to a wire rack, and serve when cooled to room temperature.

MINI RASPBERRY CROISSANTS

Mini-Croissants à la Framboise QUICKER | MAKES 24 MINI CROISSANTS

These take only 15 minutes to bake and all of 10 minutes to prepare. Make them ahead, put them in the refrigerator, and bake while family or guests are having dinner. They are a great addition to a plate of all kinds of cookies after dinner.

SPECIAL EQUIPMENT 1 BAKING SHEET LINED WITH PARCHMENT PAPER

1 package store-bought frozen puff pastry (2 sheets), thawed

½ cup raspberry jam

1 egg beaten with ½ teaspoon vanilla and ½ teaspoon water

Confectioner's sugar

Preheat oven to 400 degrees F.

On a clean, lightly floured surface, unfold 1 sheet of the pastry. With a pizza wheel, kitchen scissors, or sharp knife, cut vertically into 3 equal pieces and slice each in half horizontally. Then slice each square on a diagonal to make into triangles. Repeat with the second pastry sheet. You should have 24 triangles.

Thinly spread each triangle with 1 teaspoon raspberry jam.

Roll up each triangle snugly from the wide base to the tip at the top. Place on the baking sheet. Brush them with the egg wash then use your fingers to shape them slightly into crescents, keeping the tip tucked underneath.

Bake for 15–20 minutes, until golden. Allow to cool to room temperature then dust with confectioner's sugar.

PASTRY SHOP TRADITIONAL ALMOND PITHIVIER

Pithiviers Traditionnel aux Amandes QUICKER | SERVES 8

I was thrilled when I learned how easy this is to make at home. Normally I would buy one in the pastry shop in France, but baking it at home allows you to add a variety of ingredients to the filling depending on the season. Sometimes I add sautéed apples or pears on top of the filling, sometimes chocolate chunks. And sometimes I make it the night before then bake it in the morning for breakfast. It's as easy as making a pie, maybe easier.

SPECIAL EQUIPMENT FOOD PROCESSOR; ROLLING PIN; 1 (10-INCH) ROUND CAKE PAN; 2 BAKING SHEETS LINED WITH PARCHMENT PAPER

4 tablespoons unsalted butter

3 tablespoons granulated sugar

7 ounces almond paste, crumbled

¼ cup almond flour

1 large egg yolk

1 teaspoon almond extract

1 package store-bought frozen puff pastry (2 sheets)

1 egg yolk, beaten

4 to 6 ounces fresh raspberries

1 egg beaten with 1 teaspoon water

1 tablespoon light corn syrup

½ teaspoon water

¼ teaspoon pure vanilla extract

Prepare the filling by slicing the butter into the food processor and adding the sugar, almond paste, almond flour, egg yolk, and almond extract. Pulse 12 times then process until very smooth. Reserve.

Roll out 1 pastry sheet just a little, and using the cake pan as a template, cut around the pan with a paring knife to create a 10-inch disk of pastry. Place the disk on a baking sheet and refrigerate while you roll out the second piece.

Roll out the remaining pastry sheet and cut it 1 inch wider than the cake pan so that it will easily fit over the filling. Place this disk onto the other baking sheet and refrigerate.

Take the 10-inch circle out of the refrigerator, leaving it on the baking sheet, and place all of the filling into the center, leaving 1 inch free around the edges. Pat down the filling into a neat circle and brush the perimeter of the dough with the beaten egg yolk. Gently insert the raspberries into the filling.

Take the other disk out of the refrigerator and lay it over the top, gently pressing down all around the filling with your fingers to eliminate trapped air.

Press down all the way around to seal the edges of the pastry then trim with a knife.

Use a sharp paring knife to cut a scallop pattern all the way around the edges. Working from the center outwards, gently score decorative slits in the top of the pastry to look like the spokes of a wheel, without cutting all the way through the dough. Make a small hole in the center to let steam escape. Brush the entire pithivier with the egg wash.

Refrigerate the pithivier for 1 hour. Half an hour before baking, preheat the oven to 350 degrees F.

Bake for 20–25 minutes, until it is lightly golden. Mix the corn syrup, water, and vanilla together, lightly brush it all over the pithivier, and then return it to the oven to bake for 10–15 minutes, until it is a beautiful golden brown. Cool to room temperature, slice with a serrated knife, and serve.

TIP

If you wish, you can freeze it until you are ready to bake it. It keeps in the freezer for up to 2 weeks. Just take out of the freezer and place directly in the hot oven to bake.

APRICOT JAM SACRISTANS

Sacristains à la Confiture d'Abricots QUICKER | MAKES ABOUT 25 SACRISTANS

I spied my first sacristans displayed on a table at the open-air market in Saint-Tropez. They were gorgeous corkscrew pastries filled with a chocolaty mixture and sprinkled with finely chopped hazelnuts and powdered sugar. I like mine filled with apricot jam so it oozes out a little during baking, caramelizing and becoming crisp. Dusting with powdered sugar is optional.

SPECIAL EQUIPMENT ROLLING PIN; 2 BAKING SHEETS LINED WITH PARCHMENT PAPER

1 package store-bought frozen puff pastry (2 sheets), thawed

4 heaping tablespoons apricot jam

1 large egg beaten with 1 teaspoon water

Turbinado or crystallized sugar

1 cup confectioner's sugar, optional

Lightly sprinkle a clean work surface with flour. Roll out 1 pastry sheet to a 14-inch-long rectangle. Spread 2 tablespoons jam over the bottom half of the pastry sheet, fold over the top to cover it, and place in the refrigerator for 1 hour. Repeat with the second sheet of pastry.

Brush with the egg wash on both sides then sprinkle lightly with the turbinado sugar. With a pizza cutter, scissors, or large knife, slice each pastry into ¼-inch-wide strips.

Twist strips by holding each end and turning in opposite directions then place them about 1 inch apart on the baking sheets, pressing down at each end

to secure them to the parchment paper. Refrigerate for at least 20 minutes before baking.

Preheat the oven to 400 degrees F. Bake the sacristans for 10–12 minutes, until they are golden brown.

Take out of the oven and, when they are cool enough to handle, sprinkle with confectioner's sugar and serve.

TIP

Make the sacristans the night before, store in the refrigerator, and in the morning pop them in the oven for 10–12 minutes for fresh baked goodness to go with your coffee.

GIANT STRAWBERRY-AND-WHIPPED CREAM MILLEFEUILLE

Millefeuille Géant aux Fraises et à la Crème Fouettée **QUICKER** | SERVES 6 TO 8

Delicate, individual many-layered pastries, called millefeuille, *appear in almost every pastry shop in France. Millefeuille, which means a thousand sheets, are time consuming and a bit difficult to make.*

To make them at home, I pared the thousand sheets down to two sheets, giant ones, then sandwiched them with whipped cream and strawberries. It's a fun, big, spectacular-looking dessert to bring to the table. The light pastry, whipped cream, and fresh, ripe strawberries are delicious together. Make sure everyone is ready as it should be served immediately to preserve the volume of the whipped cream.

SPECIAL EQUIPMENT ROLLING PIN; 2 BAKING SHEETS LINED WITH PARCHMENT PAPER; ELECTRIC HAND MIXER

1 package store-bought frozen puff pastry (2 sheets)	**1 cup heavy whipping cream, chilled**	**3 tablespoons confectioner's sugar**
Confectioner's sugar	**1 teaspoon pure vanilla extract**	**1 pound strawberries, thickly sliced, plus more for garnish**

Preheat oven to 400 degrees F.

Thaw the pastry according to package instructions. On a large piece of parchment paper that has been lightly floured, roll out both sheets of pastry to 14-inch-long rectangles.

Place 1 puff pastry on each baking sheet and generously dust one of the sheets with confectioner's sugar. For both pastries, prick all over with a fork as much as possible so they don't puff up too much when baked. Place in the oven and bake for 15 minutes, or until they are golden.

Meanwhile, using the mixer, whip the cream until soft peaks form. Add the vanilla and 3 tablespoons confectioner's sugar and beat until stiff. Refrigerate until ready to use.

Remove the pastries from the oven, and while they are still warm, use a large serrated knife to slice each in half horizontally to make thinner and lighter layers. Discard the bottom halves. Put the pastry without confectioner's sugar on a serving dish with the hollowed-out side facing up.

Spoon the whipped cream onto this pastry, topping with all of the strawberries. Gently place the second pastry on top, with the sugared side facing up. Sift additional confectioner's sugar over the top and decorate with additional strawberries.

TIP

When serving, use a serrated knife to slice each piece in long gentle motions without pressing down too much.

ALSATIAN APPLE MARZIPAN STRUDEL

Strudel Alsacien aux Pommes et au Massepain LONGER | SERVES 6 TO 8

Having been passed back and forth between Germany and France for so long, Alsace developed a unique mix of German and French culture and cuisine. The apple strudels made in Germany are also made in Alsace. Classically, they take a bit of effort to make the perfect thin dough to wrap the apple filling in. For a shortcut, I use frozen ready-made puff pastry. It tastes delicious and looks even better with a dusting of confectioner's sugar.

SPECIAL EQUIPMENT ROLLING PIN; 1 BAKING SHEET LINED WITH PARCHMENT PAPER

2 tablespoons unsalted butter

1 tablespoon light brown sugar

2 large Granny Smith apples

1 store-bought frozen puff-pastry sheet, thawed

7 ounces almond paste

2 tablespoons all-purpose flour

¼ cup granulated sugar

1 tablespoon ground cinnamon

1 egg beaten with 1 teaspoon water

1 tablespoon light corn syrup

½ teaspoon water

½ teaspoon pure almond extract

Melt 2 tablespoons butter in a skillet, add the brown sugar, and stir to melt. Keep warm.

Peel and quarter the apples then slice very thinly and toss them into the skillet. Cook over medium heat for 5 minutes, until just tender. Turn off the heat.

Preheat oven to 375 degrees F.

Cut a large piece of parchment paper and flour it. Place the pastry sheet on it and roll it out to a 12 x 16-inch rectangle. Crumble the almond paste over the top, leaving 1 inch free all the way around the edge.

Sift the flour into the skillet of apples and add the sugar and cinnamon. Stir well to coat the apples.

Scoop the apples onto the short end of the pastry sheet in a long line, from end-to-end horizontally,

leaving 1 inch free at the ends. Fill all the way to the middle of the pastry sheet then, using the paper underneath the pastry as an aid to help you roll it up, begin rolling the pastry into a long log. Pinch the ends then push them underneath the log to seal. Transfer to the baking sheet, seam side down.

Brush all over with the egg wash, make slits to vent, and put into the oven to bake for 25 minutes. Meanwhile, mix the corn syrup, water, and almond extract.

After the strudel has baked for 25 minutes, remove from the oven, brush all over with the syrup mixture, and return to the oven to bake for 10–15 minutes, until golden brown. Remove from the oven and cool for 15 minutes before slicing.

SWEET VOL-AU-VENT WITH A STRAWBERRY AND TARRAGON COULIS

Vol-au-Vent Sucré, Coulis de Fraises à l'Estragon LONGER | SERVES 6

Another convenience in working with ready-made puff pastry is that you can buy ready-made puff-pastry shells, called vol-au-vent, and put almost anything into them and serve for dessert. For this recipe, I fill them with a luscious pillow of vanilla pastry cream topped with one perfect strawberry and drizzle a sweet, fresh tarragon coulis all the way around.

SPECIAL EQUIPMENT ELECTRIC STAND MIXER; FOOD PROCESSOR; 1 BAKING SHEET LINED WITH PARCHMENT PAPER

Pastry Cream

3 cups milk

3 cups half-and-half

8 large egg yolks, room temperature

1 ¼ cups granulated sugar

3 teaspoons pure vanilla extract

2 tablespoons all-purpose flour

½ cup cornstarch

4 tablespoons unsalted butter

Tarragon Coulis

1 ½ cups granulated sugar

1 ½ cups water

4 tablespoons tightly packed fresh tarragon leaves, coarsely chopped, divided

To Finish

1 package frozen puff pastry shells (vol-au-vent)

1 tablespoon unsalted butter, melted

3 tablespoons granulated sugar

6 large strawberries

PASTRY CREAM

Pour the milk and half-and-half into a saucepan and heat until small bubbles form around the edges. Turn down the heat to very low.

Using the mixer, beat together the egg yolks and sugar for 4 minutes, until they are very thick. Beat in the vanilla. Sift in the flour then cornstarch and beat to combine.

Bring the milk mixture back to almost scalding. Carefully pour a third of the hot milk into the egg mixture with the machine running.

Pour all of the egg mixture into the hot milk in the saucepan and cook over low heat while you constantly whisk. It will look frothy and thick. Do this for at least 5 minutes, as you want the pastry cream to become thick enough to hold its shape.

When you like the consistency, slice in the butter, whisking until it is all melted. Cool the pastry cream to room temperature. If you are using it later, cover with plastic wrap touching the top and place it in the refrigerator.

TARRAGON COULIS

Heat the sugar and water in a saucepan until it comes to a boil, the sugar has melted, and the mixture is clear. Add 2 tablespoons tarragon, turn heat down, and simmer for 1 minute. Turn off the heat and let steep for 15 minutes.

Add remaining tarragon leaves, pour everything into the food processor, and process until the tarragon is very finely chopped. Reserve or chill until ready to use.

TO FINISH

Preheat oven to 425 degrees F.

Place shells on baking sheet with the tops facing up. Brush them with the melted butter, sprinkle liberally with sugar, and bake for 18–20 minutes, until they are puffed and golden brown. Cool for 5 minutes before gently removing the tops with the tip of a knife.

To serve, place each vol-au-vent on a serving plate. Fill with the pastry cream, top with a strawberry, drizzle the coulis around each pastry shell, and serve.

Assiette LY

Coupes

Lunchs

..... ONNAISES

Glacées

sur Commande

TARTS

Tarts are relatively simple to make and offer you the opportunity to showcase glorious displays of fresh fruit and berries on top.

Tart crusts are a bit like cookie dough, providing a crisp shell to hold the filling. I am a tart pan junkie with a collection of tiny ones, large ones, square ones, and rectangular and circular ones, and I often double or triple a recipe so that I can fill more than one pan and freeze it for future use.

RUSTIC PLUM TART IN A SWEET FENNEL CRUST

Tarte Rustique aux Quetsches, Pâte Sucrée au Fenouil **QUICKER** | SERVES 8

I created this tart for my neighbor's birthday and remember carrying it up the hill to the table I had set under a tree where guests were waiting for a birthday cake. Instead, I set this simple tart in front of the birthday girl, who was born in Alsace. Her gasp of pleasure assured me the message was received and that she was touched to have a tart made from the area where she had grown up, in the Bas Rhine region of Alsace.

There they make a plum tart with a cinnamon-sugar streusel topping. I played with the idea a little and created a cookie-like crust with an underlying anise flavor that pairs beautifully with the soft warm plums and cinnamon-scented topping.

SPECIAL EQUIPMENT FOOD PROCESSOR; ROLLING PIN; 1 (9-INCH) TART PAN WITH REMOVABLE BOTTOM; PARCHMENT PAPER; PIE WEIGHTS

Crust

1 stick unsalted butter, chilled

¼ cup granulated sugar

1 large egg yolk

2 teaspoons fennel seeds

½ teaspoon salt

1 teaspoon pure vanilla extract

1 ½ cups all-purpose flour

2 to 4 tablespoons ice water

1 egg white beaten with
1 teaspoon water

Filling

2 pounds plums, not too ripe or soft

1 tablespoon granulated sugar

¼ teaspoon ground cinnamon

Topping

½ cup all-purpose flour or
almond flour

¼ cup granulated sugar

2 teaspoons ground cinnamon

½ stick unsalted butter, room
temperature

CRUST

Slice the butter into the food processor. Pulse 8 times then process for 5 seconds. Add the sugar, egg yolk, fennel seeds, salt, and vanilla and process for 5 seconds. Add the flour and process just until the mixture looks like sand. With the machine running, add 1 tablespoon ice water at a time, only using enough to bring the dough together. Use the least amount of water possible.

Turn out onto a large piece of plastic wrap, form into a ball, flatten into a disk, and refrigerate for 1 hour.

Roll out the dough on a clean, floured surface so that it is large enough to line the tart pan, leaving a 1-inch overhang. Fit the dough in all the way around, pressing the inside edges. Fold the dough over into the inside edges, leaving it higher than the edge of the pan because there will be a little shrinkage during baking. Pinch into a decorative pattern, cover with plastic wrap, and refrigerate for 30 minutes.

Preheat oven to 400 degrees F.

Line the tart with parchment paper, fill with pie weights, and bake for 11 minutes. Remove weights and paper, paint the bottom with the egg wash, and return to the oven to cook for another 8 minutes. Remove the tart shell from the oven, but leave the oven on at 400 degrees F. Allow the tart shell to cool down while you prepare the plums.

FILLING

Pit and quarter the plums and begin arranging them, skin side down, all the way around the outside edge of the tart shell. Continue round and round, finishing your circles in the center.

Mix the sugar and cinnamon together then sprinkle it over the plums.

TOPPING

In a bowl, whisk together the flour, sugar, and cinnamon. Add the butter and, with your fingertips, work it into the flour until it looks like sand. Sprinkle this over the top of the plums and bake for 20 minutes.

MEDIEVAL CUSTARD TART IN A CLOVE-SCENTED CRUST

Tarte Médiévale à la Crème dans une Pâte Aromatisée au Clou de Girofle

QUICKER | SERVES 8

Large, creamy custard tarts were popular in medieval France, and although it is rare to find cinnamon as an ingredient in French desserts today, it was often added then, as were cloves. This tart is flecked with lots of cinnamon and dusted with it as a finishing touch. It is an homage to desserts lost in time, and to ones that maybe should be brought back.

SPECIAL EQUIPMENT FOOD PROCESSOR; ROLLING PIN; 1 (10-INCH) TART PAN WITH REMOVABLE BOTTOM; PARCHMENT PAPER, PIE WEIGHTS; 1 BAKING SHEET

Crust

1 ¾ cups all-purpose flour or almond flour

¼ cup cornstarch

6 tablespoons granulated sugar

¼ teaspoon salt

½ teaspoon ground cloves

1 stick plus 2 tablespoons unsalted butter, chilled and cubed

1 egg beaten with 2 teaspoons pure vanilla extract

2 to 4 tablespoons ice water

Filling

4 large eggs

2 large egg yolks

½ cup granulated sugar

1 teaspoon pure vanilla extract

1 teaspoon ground cinnamon, plus more to sprinkle on top

¼ teaspoon freshly grated nutmeg, plus more to sprinkle on top

1 cup half-and-half

1 cup whipping cream

Confectioner's sugar

CRUST

Make the tart crust by adding the flour, cornstarch, sugar, salt, and cloves to the bowl of the food processor. Pulse 6 times to combine.

Add the butter and process until it resembles coarse sand. Add the beaten egg and process for 2 seconds. With the machine running, add the ice water, 1 tablespoon at a time, until the dough comes together into a ball.

Turn out the dough onto a piece of plastic wrap, bring it together into a ball, flatten down into a large flat disk, and then roll it out on a clean, floured work surface to a size larger than the tart pan, about 13 to 14 inches across. Drape the dough over the rolling pin and carry it over to the tart pan. Lay it in the tart pan and, with your fingers, gently shape it into the pan. Use kitchen scissors to cut off the excess dough, or run the rolling pin over the edges to trim. Cover and refrigerate for 1 hour.

When you are ready to bake the tart crust, preheat the oven to 375 degrees F.

Line the inside of the pastry with parchment paper and add the pie weights. Bake for 20 minutes. Remove the weights and parchment paper and bake for another 10 minutes. Remove from the oven and cool to room temperature.

Reduce the oven temperature to 325 degrees F.

FILLING

Using a large mixing bowl, add the eggs, egg yolks, granulated sugar, vanilla, cinnamon, and nutmeg and whisk to combine. Pour in the half-and-half and cream and whisk well to combine. Pour into the pastry shell, discarding any excess.

Place the tart on the baking sheet and bake for 30–40 minutes until the top is set. Remove from the oven. The cinnamon will have floated to the top of the custard. Once the tart has cooled to room temperature, sprinkle the top with cinnamon, nutmeg, and a light sifting of confectioner's sugar before slicing and serving.

TIP

If you are in a hurry, you can use a store-bought refrigerated pie crust.

STRAWBERRY PEACH GALETTE

Galette aux Fraises et aux Pêches **QUICKER** | SERVES 8

Some fruit galettes are free-form. Some are baked in a springform pan. This galette fits into any attractive baking pan or dish that you can bring to the table and serve from. Pile the center with scoops of some wonderful vanilla ice cream to melt over the hot fruit.

SPECIAL EQUIPMENT ROLLING PIN; PARCHMENT PAPER; FOOD PROCESSOR; 1 (9- OR 10-INCH) SPRINGFORM PAN; 1 BAKING SHEET

7 ounces almond paste

Pastry

2 ½ cups all-purpose flour

½ teaspoon salt

1 tablespoon granulated sugar

2 sticks unsalted butter, chilled and cut into small cubes

1 teaspoon pure vanilla extract

5 to 6 tablespoons ice water

Filling

2 cups strawberries, hulled and quartered if large, halved if smaller

2 medium-size ripe peaches with skin, cut into ¼-inch-thick slices then halved

4 tablespoons light brown sugar

4 tablespoons granulated sugar

½ teaspoon pure vanilla extract

1 teaspoon almond extract

3 ½ tablespoons cornstarch

½ teaspoon ground cinnamon

To Finish

1 egg white beaten with 1 teaspoon water

Turbinado sugar

1 quart vanilla ice cream (optional)

With your hands, shape the almond paste into a round ball then into flat disk. Roll it out between 2 sheets of parchment paper to a 9-inch circle that will fit inside your galette crust. Reserve.

PASTRY

Add the flour, salt, and sugar to the food processor and pulse 6 times to combine. Arrange the butter over the top and pulse 14 times. With the machine running, pour in the vanilla then the water, 1 tablespoon at a time, until a dough ball comes together.

Transfer the dough to a large sheet of plastic wrap. Fold over the wrap and form the dough into a ball then flatten into a large disk. Cover with a sheet of parchment paper and roll out the dough to a ½-inch-thick disk, about 14 inches across. Refrigerate for 1 hour.

Preheat the oven to 400 degrees F. Arrange a middle shelf in the oven.

FILLING

Toss the strawberries and peaches together in a bowl with the light brown and granulated sugars; let set for 30 minutes. Strain away any excess juices

and save for drizzling over the ice cream later. Add the vanilla and almond extracts to the strawberries and peaches; toss to coat. Sprinkle the cornstarch and cinnamon over the fruit and toss to thoroughly coat. Taste and add more sugar, if desired.

TO FINISH

Take the dough out of the refrigerator, drape it over a rolling pin, and transfer it to the springform pan or baking pan you have chosen. Gently fit it in, leaving the dough hanging over the sides. With kitchen scissors, trim the dough all the way around to make it a neat circle, without reducing the size very much.

Lay the almond paste disk down in the center of the dough. Heap the fruit onto the middle.

Gently pull the edges of the dough up straight then begin to overlap and pinch the edges of dough all the way around so that you cover the fruit halfway to the center. Dip your finger into the egg wash and smooth over and patch any openings in the dough, making sure to press against them to seal.

Brush the entire pastry with the egg wash then liberally sprinkle the turbinado sugar over the

pastry. Don't be shy with the sugar—the more sugar, the crunchier the crust.

Place the tart on the baking sheet and bake for 30–40 minutes, until the fruit is bubbling and the crust is golden brown.

Remove from the oven and carry to the table to serve with scoops of ice cream.

TIP

For a free-form galette, place the rolled out dough on a parchment-lined baking sheet, add the almond disk, heap your fruit in the center, pull the dough over it and pinch it together, leaving an uncovered area in the center, and then bake it per instructions. Allow to rest for 30 minutes before sliding it onto a serving plate.

CHOCOLATE ON CHOCOLATE TART WITH RASPBERRIES

Tarte Doublement Chocolat et Framboises LONGER | SERVES 8

I love adding flavors to my tart crusts, and for this one, I decided to make it taste like a crunchy chocolate sugar-and-butter cookie to contrast with the ultra-smooth truffle-like filling. Make this tart a day ahead so the ganache can firm up, and serve with fresh raspberries.

SPECIAL EQUIPMENT FOOD PROCESSOR; 1 (9-INCH) TART PAN WITH REMOVABLE BOTTOM

Pastry Crust

1 ½ cups all-purpose flour

½ teaspoon salt

½ cup granulated sugar

5 tablespoons Hershey's Special Dark Cocoa

2 teaspoons instant espresso powder

9 tablespoons unsalted butter, chilled and cubed

2 large egg yolks

1 teaspoon pure vanilla extract

2 to 3 tablespoons ice water

¼ cup raspberry jam, melted

Chocolate Ganache Filling

1 cup heavy cream

8 ounces semisweet chocolate, finely chopped

1 teaspoon pure vanilla extract

2 tablespoons unsalted butter

1 pint raspberries

PASTRY CRUST

Brush the tart pan with melted butter (you don't need to if your tart pan is nonstick).

Sift the flour into the bowl of the food processor. Add the salt, sugar, cocoa, and espresso power and pulse 6 times. Add the butter and process until granular.

With a fork, beat the egg yolks with the vanilla and add to the bowl. Process for 10 seconds then pour in 1 tablespoon water with the machine running. If the dough does not come together, add another tablespoon. Repeat up to 3 tablespoons until the dough comes together when pinched.

I usually use my fingers to press the dough into the tart tin. If it becomes sticky to work with, sprinkle some granulated sugar on the dough then press. If you would like a more perfect rendition, sprinkle granulated sugar on a clean work surface; bring the dough together into a ball with your hands, then into a disk, roll out to a size a bit larger than your tart pan, and fit into the pan.

Prick the bottom of the crust all over with a fork, cover with plastic wrap, and refrigerate for 1 hour.

Preheat oven to 375 degrees F. Bake the tart crust for 20–25 minutes, until the bottom is dry to the touch. Cool to room temperature. Paint the bottom with the raspberry jam.

CHOCOLATE GANACHE FILLING

Heat the cream in a saucepan until little bubbles form around the edges. Turn off the heat, add the chocolate and vanilla, and whisk until melted and smooth. Add the butter and whisk until combined and smooth.

Pour the ganache into the tart shell, smoothing over the top and pricking any little air bubbles. You want a very smooth surface.

Cover with a tent of aluminum foil so that it does not touch the ganache, and refrigerate for at least 4 hours or overnight.

Leave the tart on the counter to rest for 15 minutes before serving with fresh raspberries.

SWISS CHARD AND GOAT CHEESE CHEESECAKE TART

Tarte aux Blettes et au Fromage de Chèvre, comme un Cheesecake **LONGER** | SERVES 12

I lived just down the road from a couple who raised goats and sold goat cheese from their house. One day, I bought their cheese and looked over my kitchen counter at the Swiss chard I had harvested from my garden. The thought of making a cheesecake from the goat cheese came first then the thought of making a tourte de blettes *(a Niçoise sweet tart made with Swiss chard, brandy, raisins, and pine nuts) with my Swiss chard came next. What resulted was a combination of the two desserts into one. I created a goat cheese cheesecake using the cheese and local honey. And I added to it raisins and Swiss chard. What resulted has become one of my favorite tarts to make.*

SPECIAL EQUIPMENT FOOD PROCESSOR; 1 (12-INCH) NONSTICK RECTANGULAR TART PAN WITH REMOVABLE BOTTOM; PARCHMENT PAPER, PIE WEIGHTS; 1 BAKING SHEET

Crust

1 ¾ cups all-purpose flour

½ cup plus 2 tablespoons granulated sugar

½ cup confectioner's sugar

¼ teaspoon salt

1 teaspoon pure vanilla extract

1 ½ sticks unsalted butter, chilled and cubed

1 large egg, room temperature

Filling

2 stems large-leaved rainbow Swiss chard

1 ½ tablespoons light brown sugar

1 large egg, beaten

4 heaping tablespoons raisins

Cheesecake

1 (8-ounce) soft goat cheese log, room temperature

3 tablespoons honey

¼ cup plus 2 tablespoons granulated sugar

½ teaspoon anise extract

¾ teaspoon pure vanilla extract

2 large eggs, beaten

1 cup milk, room temperature

CRUST

Brush the tart pan with melted butter, sprinkle with granulated sugar, and tap out excess.

To make the crust, place the flour, granulated and confectioner's sugars, and salt into the food processor and pulse 6 times to combine. Add the vanilla and butter and process until coarsely granular. Add the egg and process until the dough starts to clump together in globs but has not yet formed a ball. Make sure it still has a pebbly texture.

Scoop the contents of the food processor into the tart shell, flour your fingers, and starting with the sides, work the dough all the way around into the edges, a little higher than the top of the pan to help prevent shrinkage. Finish pressing down the dough into the center.

continued >

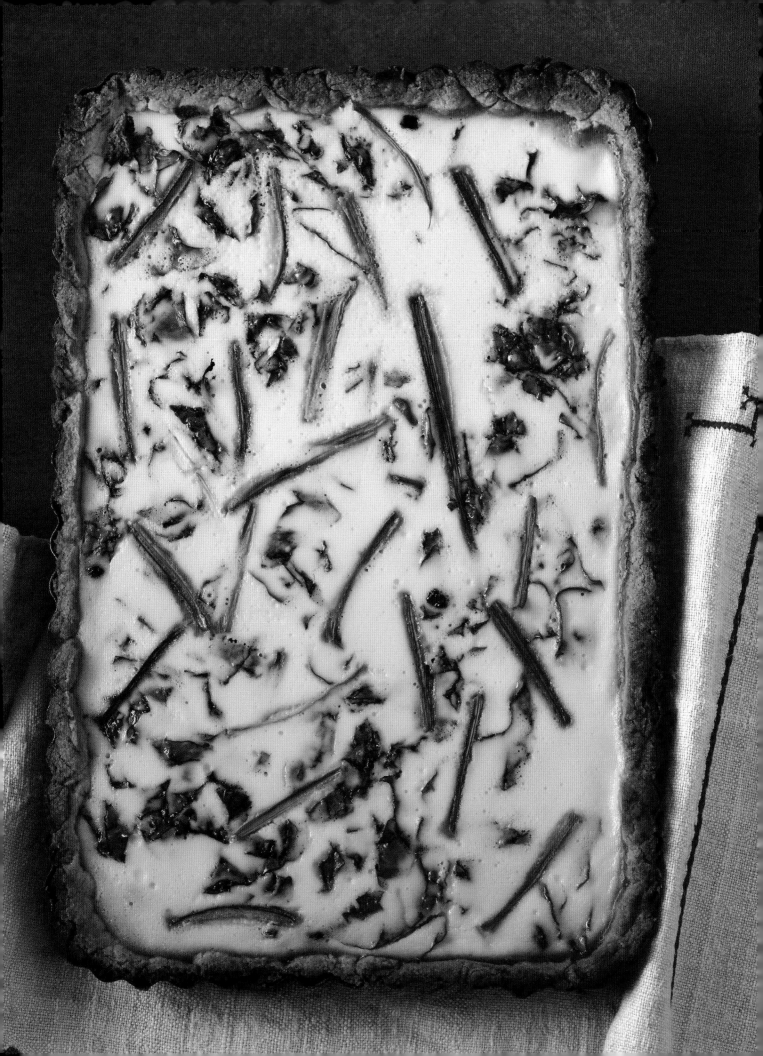

Use a fork to prick holes, not all the way through, all over the bottom of the crust. Cover with plastic wrap and refrigerate for 1 ½ hours.

Preheat the oven to 375 degrees F.

Line the tart crust with parchment paper and add pie weights, making sure they are pushed up against the sides all the way to the top edge. Bake for 10–12 minutes, until the edges begin to pull away from the tart pan. Remove the weights and parchment paper and bake for another 5 minutes to dry out the bottom. Cool to room temperature.

FILLING

Trim the leaves from the Swiss chard stems, keeping the stems. Wash and pat very dry with paper towels. Roll the leaves and slice them into ¼-inch strips. You should have 1 tightly packed cup of leaves. Toss them into a large mixing bowl. Add the brown sugar and egg and mix well. Slice the stems into thin slivers and save enough to decorate the top.

Scatter the raisins over the bottom of the tart. With your hands, squeeze the Swiss chard leaves dry to eliminate any excess sugar and egg mixture then lay them down over the raisins.

Preheat oven to 400 degrees F.

CHEESECAKE

Slice the goat cheese into the food processor, add the honey, sugar, anise, vanilla, and eggs and process until very smooth. Add the milk and process until smooth.

Place the tart pan on the baking sheet and cover the tart edges with strips of aluminum foil to protect them from browning too much.

Pour the cheesecake filling over the chard layer in the tart shell, decorate the top with the chard stems, and bake for 30–35 minutes, until it is slightly puffed and golden around the edges.

Cool to room temperature before unmolding and serving.

TIP

You can make the crust earlier in the day and finish the filling later, or make it a day ahead and keep in the refrigerator until you are ready to fill and bake it.

CANDIES AND

MIGNARDISES

═══════════════════════════════════════

Don't you love it when a restaurant surprises you with an arrangement of small sweets at the end of your meal? In France, these can include tiny cookies, candies, or bite-size pastries. In this chapter I've included recipes for making your own *mignardises* plate.

WHITE CHOCOLATE TRUFFLES WITH DRIED CHERRIES AND CHOCOLATE WHISKEY TRUFFLES

Des Truffes Chocolat Blanc et Cerises Séchées et des Truffes Chocolat et Whiskey

QUICKER | MAKES 24 (1-INCH) TRUFFLES OF EACH FLAVOR

You can serve these in small foil candy cups or simply scatter them across a beautiful platter with a dusting of cocoa. Homemade truffles are always on my menu when I entertain, even if I just tuck a couple on the saucer next to everyone's espresso.

SPECIAL EQUIPMENT 1 SMALL MELON BALLER; PARCHMENT PAPER

White Truffles

5 tablespoons heavy cream

11 ounces white chocolate chips

1 teaspoon pure anise extract

¼ teaspoon salt

½ cup dried cherries, chopped

Confectioner's sugar

Chocolate Whiskey Truffles

3 tablespoons heavy cream

⅛ teaspoon salt

8 ounces semisweet chocolate, finely chopped

3 tablespoons unsalted butter

1 heaping teaspoon Hershey's Special Dark Cocoa

2 tablespoons plus 1 teaspoon whiskey

Hershey's Special Dark Cocoa

WHITE TRUFFLES

In a saucepan, heat the cream until small bubbles form around the edges and it begins to simmer. Take it off the heat, pour in the chocolate chips, and stir until melted. Stir in the anise, salt, and dried cherries.

Scoop mixture into a shallow bowl, cover with plastic wrap, and refrigerate for 1 hour, or until firm.

Use the melon baller or small spoon to make balls, about 1 inch across. Drop them onto parchment paper covered with confectioner's sugar and roll into smooth balls. Toss the truffles into a plastic bag and into the refrigerator or freezer until ready to serve.

CHOCOLATE WHISKEY TRUFFLES

In a saucepan, heat the cream until small bubbles form around the edges and it begins to simmer. Add salt, chocolate, and butter and stir until smooth. Add the cocoa and stir until smooth. Finally, add the whiskey and stir until smooth. Pour into a small bowl and place in the freezer for 1 hour, or until firm.

Use the melon baller or small spoon to make balls, about 1 inch across. Drop them onto parchment paper covered with cocoa and roll into smooth balls. Toss the truffles into a plastic bag and into the refrigerator or freezer until ready to serve.

MINI PAIN D'ÉPICES

Mini-Pains d'Épices **QUICKER** | MAKES 24 PIECES

I used to climb and climb and climb up hairpin turns to the village above mine, perched in the clouds, to visit a shop that made some of the best pain d'épices, *a French spiced gingerbread, I had ever tasted. Now I replicate that ethereal flavor and texture in a mini version with the following recipe.*

Traditionally, pain d'épices *are made with some rye flour, which can be hard to find, so use all-purpose flour. I dip these little wonders in melted butter and add a bit of crunch with the spiced sugar on top.*

SPECIAL EQUIPMENT 2 MINI MUFFIN TINS

Mini pain d'épices

2 ½ cups all-purpose flour

1 teaspoon baking powder

¼ teaspoon salt

6 cracks freshly ground black pepper

1 teaspoon ground cumin

2 tablespoons ground cinnamon

2 teaspoons ground ginger

2 large eggs, room temperature

¼ cup honey

½ cup plus 3 tablespoons granulated sugar

½ cup dark brown sugar

½ cup organic orange juice

¼ cup milk

1 teaspoon pure vanilla extract

Topping

¼ cup granulated sugar

1 tablespoon ground cinnamon

1 teaspoon ground ginger

¼ cup butter, melted

MINI PAIN D'ÉPICES

Preheat oven to 350 degrees F. Butter and flour the mini muffin tins.

In a large mixing bowl, sift together the flour, baking powder, salt, pepper, cumin, cinnamon, and ginger.

In another bowl, whisk the eggs then add in the honey, granulated sugar, and brown sugar and whisk to combine. Add the orange juice, milk, and vanilla and whisk well.

Add the dry ingredients to the wet ingredients and stir until just combined, being careful not to overmix. Fill the mini muffin cups ½ to ⅔ full and

bake for 15 minutes. Cool in the pans then turn out onto wire racks to cool.

TOPPING

Whisk the sugar, cinnamon, and ginger together. Dip the tops of each mini pain d'épices in the melted butter then in the sugar and spice mixture so they have an even coating. Wait 1 hour before serving them for the topping to become crunchy.

TIP

Double the recipe, pop them in a plastic freezer bag, and have them on hand to use as needed.

EASY ORANGETTES WITH CHOCOLATE SQUIGGLES

Orangettes Faciles Zébrées de Chocolat QUICKER | MAKES APPROXIMATELY 18 PEELS

Once I learned how to make these, I never looked back. My trick is to make them in the microwave. I actually prefer the taste and texture produced with this technique, rather than cooking them on the stovetop. It is so much easier that I find myself making them more frequently. They make great last-minute gifts.

This recipe is for making a small batch of approximately 18 peels. The same technique works for making grapefruit and lemon peels. Contrary to most recipes that involve lengthy and repeated cooking and draining to reduce the amount of bitterness in the peel, I like mine with a bitter orange tang paired with the crunchy sugar coating. This technique achieves that as well. An added bonus with this recipe is that I can make fresh marmalade for the next morning's breakfast with the leftover sugar syrup and orange. Simply slice the orange into the syrup and cook it at a rapid simmer until the mixture thickens then refrigerate.

SPECIAL EQUIPMENT PARCHMENT PAPER

Orangettes	Chocolate Drizzle
1 medium to large organic orange	$\frac{1}{3}$ cup heavy cream
Water	3 ounces semisweet chocolate
2 cups granulated sugar, divided	$\frac{1}{2}$ teaspoon orange extract

ORANGETTES

Thoroughly wash and dry the orange. With a small paring knife, slice off the peel from one end of the orange to the other in large pieces. Most recipes ask you to slice off the white pith, but I like to use the pith, so leave it on and use as much of it as you like because it makes thicker, chewier orangettes. You can also square the orange peel pieces off by slicing off the ends, but I like mine to have random shapes.

Drop the slices of peel into a microwave-safe container, cover with water, and microwave for 2 minutes. Drain.

Slice the peels into long strips about $\frac{1}{8}$ to $\frac{1}{4}$ inch wide and toss back into the container. Add $\frac{1}{2}$ cup sugar and toss the peels to coat. And another $\frac{1}{2}$ cup sugar and $\frac{1}{3}$ cup water, cover, and microwave for 4 minutes. Allow to rest in the microwave for 2 minutes.

Spread remaining sugar over a piece of parchment paper. Lift a few of the peels at a time with a fork onto the sugar and toss them around to coat. Place them on a wire rack with parchment paper underneath and continue with the remaining peels. The peels will be dry and hardened within 1 hour.

CHOCOLATE DRIZZLE

Heat the cream in a saucepan until little bubbles appear around the edges. Toss in the chocolate and orange extract and stir until melted and smooth. Test if it is liquid enough by dipping fork tines into it and waving the fork above a plate. If it needs to be thinner, add a touch more cream and try again.

Dip the fork tines into the chocolate drizzle and wave it back and forth over the dried orangettes.

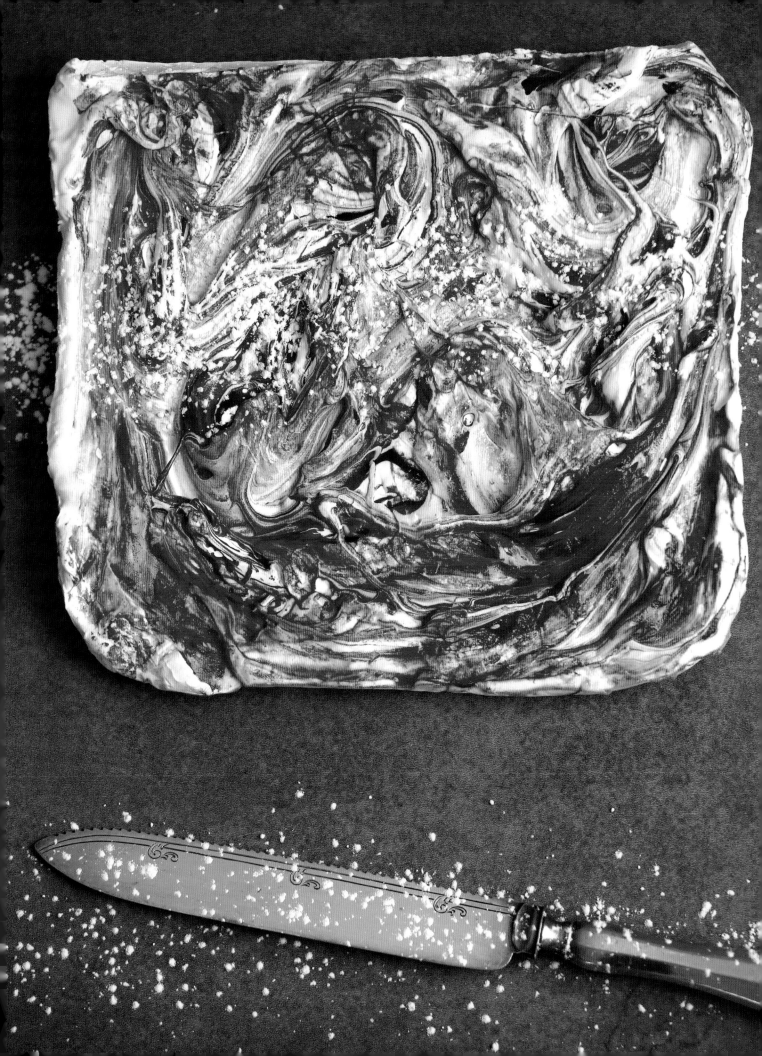

SWIRLY MARSHMALLOWS

Guimauves Marbrées **LONGER** | AMOUNT DEPENDS ON SIZES OF MARSHMALLOWS

There was a pastry shop in Antibes that displayed huge squares of white marshmallows that fascinated me but never tempted me enough to go in and try them. Then a friend told me they were the most ethereal marshmallows she ever had. So I walked in. Wow. The difference between what I knew as packaged marshmallows from the supermarket and what I tasted when those clouds melted in my mouth was a totally different experience.

Ever since then, I make my own using all sorts of flavors such as fennel, cardamom, orange or lemon extracts, vanilla bean, espresso, liqueurs, or dried fruit.

The French adore marshmallows, called guimauve, *which usually are presented as gorgeous large cubes in a variety of colors and flavors that you enjoy as a candy or snack. They even come in long, thin rectangular ropes. If you would like fun shapes, try piping the mixture into animal-shaped silicone molds found at craft or kitchen stores.*

SPECIAL EQUIPMENT 1 (8 X 8-INCH) SQUARE BAKING PAN; ELECTRIC STAND MIXER WITH WHISK ATTACHMENT; CANDY OR DIGITAL THERMOMETER

½ cup plus ¼ cup cold water

3 packets unflavored powdered gelatin

2 cups granulated sugar

⅔ cup light corn syrup

¼ teaspoon salt

2 teaspoons pure vanilla extract

1 or 2 drops red food coloring, optional

1 cup confectioner's sugar

½ cup cornstarch

Colored sugar

Line the baking pan with plastic wrap and leave the ends long enough that they hang over the sides so you can use them as a sling to remove the marshmallow when it is done. Spray with cooking spray.

Pour ½ cup cold water in the bowl of your stand mixer and sprinkle the gelatin over the top. Stir then allow to set for 8 minutes.

Meanwhile, add ¼ cup water, sugar, and corn syrup to a small saucepan and bring to a boil, being careful not to let it boil over. Turn off the heat. When the gelatin is ready, bring this mixture back to a boil then turn off the heat. (You don't need to, but if you wish, you can use a candy thermometer at this point. When the boiling syrup reaches 238 degrees F, it is ready to use.)

Start the stand mixer on low speed then carefully pour the boiling sugar syrup into the softened gelatin, turning the mixer up to high speed once it is all in. Add salt and continue to beat at medium-high speed for about 7 minutes, or until it is thick and glossy. Add the vanilla and beat again for 1 minute to incorporate.

continued >

Spray a rubber spatula with cooking spray and use it to scoop the marshmallow mixture into the prepared pan. Dip the spatula into water and smooth out the marshmallow in the pan and level the top. Add 1 or 2 drops red food coloring, if you wish, and swirl into the marshmallow all the way to the bottom.

Sift together the confectioner's sugar with the cornstarch then sift over the top of the marshmallow, keeping some to use later.

Leave the marshmallow to rest for at least 1 hour, or more, so that it firms up.

Liberally sift confectioner's sugar over a cutting board. Take the plastic wrap handles and pull up to dislodge the marshmallow and invert it onto the cutting board. Pull away the plastic wrap. Liberally sift the remaining confectioner's sugar and cornstarch mixture all over the marshmallow then use kitchen scissors, a pizza cutter, or a sharp knife lightly sprayed with cooking oil to cut the marshmallow into shapes. Dredge each shape again with confectioner's sugar mixture.

If you would like to pipe the shapes instead of putting them in the pan, use a pastry bag or gallon ziplock bag (which you have cut a corner and fitted a piping tip into) and fill as much as possible with the marshmallow mixture. Pipe out shapes onto a piece of parchment paper. Mine are usually a couple of inches across, but you can make them as large as you like.

If you would like to form more rustic random shapes that look like clouds, spray 2 large spoons with cooking spray then spoon out the marshmallow mixture onto the parchment paper in random shapes, mounding them high.

At this point, you can sprinkle them with colored sugar and let them rest for 1 hour. Then put confectioner's sugar into a bowl and toss each marshmallow all around to coat. They are ready to serve or can be stored in airtight containers for up to 1 week.

NONNETTES

Les Nonnettes **LONGER** | MAKES 12 NONNETTES

Nonnettes *means little nuns, as they were originally made by nuns in the Middle Ages. Small cakes with orange marma-*
lade hidden in the center, they are mainly found in the area around Dijon but can sometimes be found in other areas of the
country.

SPECIAL EQUIPMENT 1 MINI MUFFIN TIN

Nonnettes

½ cup all-purpose flour

1 ½ cups whole-wheat flour

1 teaspoon baking soda

2 teaspoons baking powder

2 tablespoons ground cinnamon

½ teaspoon ground ginger

¼ teaspoon ground cloves

2 large eggs

½ cup plus 2 tablespoons milk

¼ cup plus 3 tablespoons dark
  brown sugar

¼ cup honey

¾ cup orange marmalade

Glaze

2 tablespoons confectioner's
  sugar

1 teaspoon water

NONNETTES

Preheat oven to 350 degrees F. Butter and flour the mini muffin tin.

Sift both flours into a large mixing bowl. Add the baking soda, baking powder, cinnamon, ginger, and cloves and whisk to combine.

In another bowl, add the eggs, milk, brown sugar, and honey and whisk to combine. Add the wet ingredients to the dry ingredients and stir until just combined, without overmixing.

Fill the muffin cups only ¼ full. Drop 1 level teaspoon marmalade onto the top of each cup, cover with just enough batter to fill each muffin cup ½ to ⅔ full, and bake for 20 minutes. Let cool for 5 minutes then remove from pan.

GLAZE

Make a thick paste with the confectioner's sugar and water; while the muffins are still warm, spread glaze over the tops.

TIP

Instead of orange marmalade, you could give the nonnettes a heart of Nutella.

ALMOND-BROWN BUTTER FINANCIERS

Financiers aux Amandes et au Beurre Noisette **LONGER** | MAKES 15 FINANCIERS

These little cakes, invented in the late 1800s, were named financiers *because they were created by a baker who was located near the financial district of Paris. Financiers are normally baked into rectangular shapes in a special financier baking pan. Instead, I recommend that you make them in a mini muffin tin.*

The simple elegance of these little beauties, the nutty taste of brown butter, and the variety of texture from crispy on the outside to soft on the inside is irresistible. This is one of my most prized recipes.

SPECIAL EQUIPMENT 2 MINI MUFFIN TINS PLACED ON BAKING SHEETS

¼ cup all-purpose flour

¼ teaspoon salt

½ cup plus 3 tablespoons almond flour

½ cup granulated sugar

⅓ cup confectioner's sugar

1 teaspoon almond extract

3 large egg whites, room temperature

1 stick unsalted butter

Confectioner's sugar, optional

Preheat oven to 400 degrees F. Butter and flour the mini muffin tins.

In a large mixing bowl, sift in the all-purpose flour and salt. Add the almond flour, granulated sugar, and confectioner's sugar and whisk well to combine.

In another bowl, whisk the almond extract into the egg whites until just frothy.

In a saucepan, melt the butter over low heat then bring the heat up to medium and let simmer, without stirring, for 3–5 minutes, until the milk solids have gone to the bottom and have begun to turn light brown. You will hear it gurgle and snap as it cooks and begins to turn amber. Watch carefully as you do not want it to turn a dark brown. You just made a *beurre noisette,* or brown butter.

Add the dry ingredients to the egg white mixture and whisk until combined. While the butter is still

hot, pour it through a fine mesh strainer into a bowl and measure out ½ cup. Pour this into the batter and whisk just until it is combined and smooth.

Fill the muffin tins to the top with batter, lower the oven heat to 350 degrees F, and bake for 13–15 minutes, until they have risen in the center, the exterior is golden brown, and the edges are darker brown.

Cool in the tins then remove the muffins to a wire rack to cool completely. I serve them plain, but you can also lightly dust the tops with confectioner's sugar.

TIP

I've seen these with the addition of mini chocolate chips, pistachios, hazelnuts, cocoa powder, orange flower water, a drop of lemon curd, minced fresh mint or basil, or espresso. Frozen berries work as well.

SPECIAL OCCASION DESSERTS

These are the dessert recipes I make when I have company or plan a family celebration. They are indeed a bit more special, a bit more showy, and fun.

The epitome of elegance, my pear charlotte (page 198) will elicit gasps of delight with each creamy bite. For a quick yet stunning rendition of apple pie, try making Pastis Gascon (page 196). There's also a recipe for an impressive Pavlova (page 193) topped with berries and whipped cream, one for a glamorous multi-layer almond tart (page 201), and one for a rum-soaked Baba au Rhum (page 205) large enough to feed a crowd. The White Chocolate Crèmes Brûlées with Salty Pistachios (page 195) are smile-inducing individual servings, while the puffy classic Chocolate Soufflé (page 194) can star after a romantic dinner for two. And finally, there is a dessert I created when I lived in France and continue to make, inspired by the gelées the French make during the summer. Mine is all chocolate, formed into a glossy modernist square then topped with a mountain of berries and whipped cream.

PAVLOVA WITH MIXED BERRIES

Pavlova aux Fruits Rouges QUICKER | SERVES 4 TO 6

One evening in Provence we visited a restaurant where we sat outside to dine at long wooden tables set under the trees. Our dessert was an amazing white and pink Pavlova, a crisp-on-the-outside and creamy-on-the-inside ivory meringue shell filled with raspberry purée mixed into whipped cream and topped with more raspberries. Although Pavlova is a dessert from New Zealand, it is a popular dessert for French families to make to showcase seasonal fresh fruit. I also love it, and it now makes a regular appearance on my summer table.

SPECIAL EQUIPMENT 1 BAKING SHEET; PARCHMENT PAPER; ELECTRIC STAND MIXER WITH WHISK ATTACHMENT

Pavlova

8 large egg whites, room temperature

2 cups superfine sugar

2 level tablespoons cornstarch, sifted

2 teaspoons white vinegar

Whipped Cream

1 ½ cups heavy whipping cream, chilled

½ teaspoon pure vanilla extract

6 tablespoons confectioner's sugar

To serve

Mixed berries

PAVLOVA

Line the baking sheet with parchment paper. Draw an 8-inch circle then turn the parchment paper over. Preheat the oven to 200 degrees F.

Make sure the bowl of your stand mixer and its whisk are very clean and dry. Beat egg whites in the mixer on medium low for 1 minute. Turn up the speed to medium high and beat the egg whites until they begin to form stiff peaks.

Whisk the sugar and cornstarch together in a bowl. Gradually sprinkle it into the egg whites with the machine running until stiff peaks form and it is glossy. Your machine will sound like it is working hard. Add the vinegar and whisk in by hand until combined.

Scoop the meringue onto the circle on the parchment paper and use a silicon spatula to form it into a round free-form shape, making it as high as possible as it will settle back down during baking.

Bake for 1 hour. I like my Pavlova spongy and moist inside, so I cook mine less than usual. If you like yours drier inside, cook it for 1 hour and 20 minutes. Turn off the heat in the oven, leave the oven door cracked open by putting a wooden spoon in between the door and the oven, and leave the meringue there for 1 hour to completely cool. It is normal for cracks to form.

WHIPPED CREAM

Beat the cream until soft peaks form. Add the vanilla and sugar and beat again until stiff peaks form. Spoon this onto the top of the Pavlova and serve with mixed berries showered over the top.

TIP

Don't make a Pavlova when it is humid or raining outside, as it will not work as well. Make it on sunny, dry days.

CHOCOLATE SOUFFLÉ

Soufflé au Chocolat QUICKER | SERVES 4

Because of my father's love for soufflés and his enthusiasm for frequently making them, I learned at an early age there is nothing to fear. Yes, they will fall if you open the oven door before they are ready. Yes, they will deflate if you don't eat them right away. But once you know that, there's no stopping you from making them.

SPECIAL EQUIPMENT 1 (8-INCH) SOUFFLÉ DISH; PARCHMENT PAPER; KITCHEN TWINE; ROASTING PAN; ELECTRIC HAND MIXER

1 ½ tablespoons unsalted butter, softened

Granulated sugar

2 (4-ounce) bars semisweet chocolate, finely chopped

¼ cup milk

4 tablespoons unsalted butter

4 tablespoons all-purpose flour

1 ¼ cups half-and-half

3 teaspoons pure vanilla extract

4 egg yolks, room temperature

¼ cup granulated sugar

5 egg whites, room temperature

½ teaspoon cream of tartar

Confectioner's sugar

Arrange a rack in the oven that will leave enough room for the soufflé dish to fit in with its high paper collar.

Preheat oven to 375 degrees F. Use 1 tablespoon butter to grease the inside of the soufflé dish then sprinkle all over with granulated sugar.

Cut 1 piece of parchment 26 inches long by 11 inches high and fold it in half horizontally. Butter the upper half of the paper with ½ tablespoon butter and liberally sprinkle it with granulated sugar. Wrap the paper around the dish and tie it with twine so that the paper extends 4 inches above the rim of the dish. This gives the soufflé a surface to climb.

Place the dish in the roasting pan. Heat enough water to fill the roasting pan halfway; keep the water hot until needed.

Melt the chocolate with the milk in a saucepan over low heat, whisking until smooth.

Melt the 4 tablespoons butter in a separate saucepan, whisk in the flour, and cook for 2 minutes. Add the half-and-half gradually as you whisk. Add the vanilla and cook until thickened. Whisk in the melted chocolate and allow to cool to room temperature.

Using the hand mixer, beat the egg yolks with the ¼ cup granulated sugar until they are pale and thick. Whisk in the chocolate mixture to blend.

Clean the beaters then beat the egg whites until foamy in a separate bowl. Add the cream of tartar and beat until stiff.

Add 1 cup of the egg whites to the chocolate mixture and whisk gently to lighten the batter. Then add all of the egg whites and, using a rubber spatula, cut down with the edge of the spatula into the mixture and scoop the batter upwards. Turn the bowl and repeat all the way around, folding the bottom batter into the top. You do this rather than stirring so you maintain as much volume as possible.

Scoop all of the batter into the soufflé dish. Run your thumb around the inside edge of the dish to help it rise.

Place the roasting pan with the soufflé dish in the oven. Carefully pour hot water into the roasting pan to reach halfway up the soufflé dish. Bake for 35–40 minutes, or until puffy. Check visually, without opening the oven door, at 25 minutes, and only open and take the soufflé out when it is fully puffed up and ready to remove from the oven.

Remove the paper collar. Dust the top of the soufflé with confectioner's sugar and serve.

WHITE CHOCOLATE CRÈMES BRÛLÉES WITH SALTY PISTACHIOS

Crèmes Brûlées au Chocolat Blanc et aux Pistaches Salées QUICKER | SERVES 6

No need for a blowtorch to make these easy individual crèmes brûlées. *I make the caramel in a skillet and pour it over each dessert. It hardens into a beautiful mahogany hard surface that you punch through with your spoon to reach the cool, creamy custard below.*

SPECIAL EQUIPMENT 6 (8-OUNCE) RAMEKINS; ROASTING PAN

4 large egg yolks, room temperature

2 large eggs, room temperature

⅛ teaspoon salt

¼ cup plus 2 tablespoons granulated sugar

3 cups heavy cream

1 vanilla bean

6 ounces white chocolate, finely chopped

2 teaspoons pure vanilla extract

Caramel Topping

1 cup granulated sugar

1 cup salted shelled pistachios, coarsely chopped

Preheat oven to 300 degrees F. Place the ramekins in the roasting pan. Heat enough water to reach halfway up the ramekins so that it is very hot by the time you are ready to bake.

In a heatproof bowl, whisk the egg yolks and eggs with the salt and sugar until blended.

In a saucepan, heat the cream until small bubbles form around the edges and it is almost at a simmer. Scrape in the vanilla bean seeds and then toss in the bean. Add the chocolate, remove from heat, and vigorously stir until melted. Whisk in the vanilla until the mixture is very smooth.

Pour the hot cream mixture very slowly into the eggs while continuously whisking. Slowly adding the hot cream to the eggs tempers the eggs and slowly raises their temperature before entering the hot oven. Pull out the vanilla bean and discard. Fill the ramekins with this mixture.

Put the roasting pan into the oven then carefully pour in the hot water until it comes halfway up each ramekin. Bake for 25–30 minutes, until set.

Remove from the oven (being careful not to slosh water from the baking dish into the ramekins) and cool to room temperature. Then cover them with plastic wrap and refrigerate.

Take them out of the refrigerator 30 minutes before serving.

CARAMEL TOPPING

Place a skillet over low to medium heat, pour in sugar, and periodically shake until the sugar has melted and turned a deep caramel color. Very carefully, so as not to splash the hot caramel on your skin, spoon it over each custard and swirl to completely cover the tops. Sprinkle with pistachios and let set for 2 minutes, until the caramel has hardened and is ready to serve.

PASTIS GASCON

Le Pastis Gascon LONGER | SERVES 6 TO 8

A sweet from the southwest of France, pastis gascon is quite difficult to make, as it requires paper-thin dough that needs lots of gentle pulling to stretch it into very thin pieces, so many people use store-bought phyllo to make it at home. It also requires marinating apples in Armagnac overnight. The tart is quick to make the next day and looks marvelous with all its ruffles.

SPECIAL EQUIPMENT 1 (9- OR 10-INCH) TART PAN WITH REMOVABLE BOTTOM OR 1 PIE PLATE

First Day

3 tablespoons butter

6 medium to large Granny Smith apples

2 tablespoons granulated sugar

½ cup light brown sugar

1 teaspoon pure vanilla extract

½ cup Armagnac or cognac

Second Day

10 sheets phyllo dough

6 tablespoons butter, melted

½ cup confectioner's sugar, divided

FIRST DAY

Melt butter in a skillet. Peel and core the apples, slice into quarters then into paper-thin slices, and toss in the skillet. Sprinkle the granulated sugar over the top and cook the apples on low heat until they are just barely soft. Turn off the heat and let the apples cool to room temperature.

In a large mixing bowl, whisk the brown sugar, vanilla, and Armagnac to combine.

Toss the apples into the bowl and stir well to coat. Cover with plastic wrap and let set on the counter overnight. Check the instructions on the frozen phyllo dough. If it needs to thaw overnight in the refrigerator, put the package in the refrigerator.

SECOND DAY

Preheat the oven to 400 degrees F. Butter the tart pan.

Dry the apples in paper towels and discard any leftover juice or sugar in the bowl.

Lay 1 sheet of phyllo in the pan. Brush lightly with melted butter and sprinkle with confectioner's sugar. Repeat for 2 more sheets of phyllo, laying each sheet perpendicular to the last.

Mound half the apples on the phyllo, sprinkle with confectioner's sugar, mound the remaining apples on top, and sprinkle with more sugar.

Lay 1 sheet of phyllo over the top, brush lightly with melted butter, and sprinkle lightly with confectioner's sugar. Repeat for 1 more sheet of phyllo. Fold in all the edges very loosely over the apples.

With kitchen shears, cut the last 5 pieces of phyllo and scatter, interweave, and ruffle them across the top, attempting to pile them high and leave space between them.

Bake for 25 minutes, or until light golden brown.

Lightly dust with confectioner's sugar and serve. The pastis gascon will be thin and very light. It is best served while still warm out of the oven. If you must serve it later or the next day, reheat it in the oven to crisp it up.

TIP

Have a little fun with this and make individual free-form desserts by placing smaller circles of phyllo on a baking sheet, adding the apples, then pulling up the phyllo on all sides to make purses.

A PRECIOUS PEAR CHARLOTTE

Une Adorable Charlotte aux Poires LONGER | SERVES 8

First created in France by the great chef Antonin Carême, a charlotte was a creation of sliced cake lining a mold then filled with a mousse thickened with gelatin. It is a classic French pastry, brought to the table tied around the middle with a satin ribbon. Normally the French would buy this in a pastry shop, but it is actually quite easy to make at home, although it requires several steps, takes time, and must be made the day before as it needs to be refrigerated overnight. It's totally worth it.

SPECIAL EQUIPMENT 1 (7.5- TO 8-INCH) GLASS OR CERAMIC SOUFFLÉ DISH OR A TRADITIONAL CHARLOTTE MOLD; FOOD PROCESSOR; ELECTRIC HAND MIXER

Charlotte

1 cup plus ¾ cup granulated sugar, divided

1 ¼ cup plus 1 tablespoon dry white wine, divided

4 star anise

3 (15-ounce) cans sliced pears in syrup or pear juice

1 ½ cups heavy whipping cream, chilled

¼ teaspoon anise extract

6 large egg yolks, room temperature

1 tablespoon unflavored powdered gelatin

1 (7-ounce) package Savoiardi biscuits or ladyfingers

Melted Chocolate

½ cup heavy cream

¼ teaspoon salt

4 ounces semisweet chocolate, finely chopped

CHARLOTTE

Cut a piece of plastic wrap 24 inches long and fit it into the dish or mold, leaving the excess hanging as you will use it later to fold over the top. Cut off another piece of plastic wrap and fit it into the dish at a 90-degree angle. Gently press all the way around the bottom to ensure the plastic wrap fits snugly. The plastic wrap will ensure that the charlotte is easy to unmold.

Make a wine syrup by melting 1 cup sugar with 1 cup wine and the star anise in a saucepan. Bring to a boil, reduce to a simmer, and cook for 5 minutes. Cool to room temperature then discard the star anise.

Drain the pears, reserving the syrup. Put 2 ½ cups of the pears in the food processor and process until

very smooth. Measure out 1 ½ cups of the purée. Save the rest of the pears for later.

Using the mixer, whip the cream and the anise extract until soft peaks form. Refrigerate until ready to use.

Pour ¾ cup sugar over the egg yolks then beat for 3 minutes until fluffy and pale. Combine the pear purée and ¼ cup wine in a saucepan and bring to a boil, being careful not to let it plop on your skin.

Soften the gelatin in 8 teaspoons pear syrup, stir, let rest for 5 minutes, and then add it to the boiling pear purée. Whisk while simmering for 1 minute then take off the heat and continue whisking for 4 minutes.

continued >

Scoop half of the pear mixture into the egg yolks and beat for 30 seconds then add the rest of the mixture and beat for 1 minute. Allow to cool for 10 minutes. If it is too warm, it will deflate the whipped cream.

Quickly dip the biscuits into the wine syrup and line them up around the inside edges of the mold with their rounded sides out. Then line the bottom with them. Keep any remaining wine syrup.

Fold the whipped cream into the egg mixture, trying to maintain volume while thoroughly combining.

Pour this mixture into the mold, fold over the plastic wrap to cover the top, and place in the refrigerator overnight.

The next day, when you are ready to serve the charlotte, use a small sharp knife or kitchen scissors to cut off the tops of the cookies so they are flush with the chilled custard. Fit a plate over the charlotte and invert to unmold. Pull the mold off the charlotte and take off the plastic wrap. Arrange the reserved pear slices in a decorative pattern over the top.

MELTED CHOCOLATE

Make the chocolate drizzle by heating the cream and salt in a saucepan until small bubbles form around the edges. Toss in the chocolate, remove from heat, and vigorously whisk until the chocolate is melted and the drizzle is smooth. Drizzle over the top of the pears and serve the charlotte.

TIP

For festive occasions, tie a beautiful ribbon around the charlotte: white for a wedding theme, red for Christmas, orange for Thanksgiving, pink for Valentine's Day.

VALBONNAISE ALMOND TART

Tarte Valbonnaise aux Amandes **LONGER** | SERVES 8

Invented by the French pastry chef Christian Camprini, the Valbonnaise *is named after the village of Valbonne, which is down the hill from where I lived in France My rendition of his dazzling tart is vastly simplified, yet comes out tasting and looking pretty close to the original.*

It is made in three layers—a shortbread layer, a marzipan layer, and a baked layer of almond meringue topped with sliced almonds that have been caramelized while they bake—yielding different textures, from the crunchy bottom all the way up to the soft, chewy top layer.

SPECIAL EQUIPMENT 1 (9-INCH) SPRINGFORM PAN; PARCHMENT PAPER; ELECTRIC STAND MIXER

Shortbread Layer

Softened butter and sugar, for the pan

2 sticks unsalted butter, room temperature

¾ cup granulated sugar

½ teaspoon salt

1 teaspoon pure vanilla extract

1 ½ cups all-purpose flour

½ cup cornstarch

Marzipan Layer

¼ cup orange marmalade

1 (7-ounce) package almond paste

Zest of 1 organic orange

Almond Meringue Layer

5 large egg whites, room temperature

1 teaspoon vanilla

¼ teaspoon cream of tartar

¼ teaspoon salt

1 cup confectioner's sugar

¾ cup almond flour

½ cup or more sliced almonds

Confectioner's sugar

SHORTBREAD LAYER

Preheat the oven to 325 degrees F. Butter and sugar the bottom of the springform pan. Cut a piece of parchment paper that will be long enough to stand up and line the inside of the pan all the way around, approximately 29 inches long and 3 inches high when folded in half. Butter and generously sugar the paper and stand it up around the inside of the pan.

Using the mixer, cream the butter and sugar for 2 minutes. Add the salt, vanilla, flour, and cornstarch and then pinch and knead with your hands until you have a soft dough. Scoop all of this into the bottom of the pan and press down into an even layer using your fingers. Wet your fingers and smooth it out along the edges and across the middle. Refrigerate for 30 minutes.

Bake the shortbread for 35–45 minutes, until lightly golden and darker around the edges. Cool to room temperature then place in the freezer while you make the rest of the layers.

MARZIPAN LAYER

Melt the marmalade. Grate the almond paste into a bowl, add the marmalade and orange zest, and mix well with a fork to combine. Spread this on the shortbread layer.

ALMOND MERINGUE LAYER

Beat the egg whites and vanilla with the cream of tartar and salt until soft peaks form. Gradually add 1 cup sugar and beat until stiff. Sprinkle in the almond flour and mix on low for 30 seconds. Spread evenly over the marzipan layer.

Sprinkle all of the sliced almonds over the top then lightly dust with confectioner's sugar.

Bake for 55 minutes. Remove from oven and let cool for 2 minutes then unmold the cake from the pan. Cool completely before slicing and serving.

SILKY CHOCOLATE JELLY WITH BERRIES AND WHIPPED CREAM

Gelée Soyeuse au Chocolat, Fruits Rouges et Crème Fouettée **LONGER** | SERVES 8 TO 10

The French love making gelée in the summer, which are typically formed in loaf pans and are full of fruits of the season. I've indulged in my love for chocolate by instead creating a gelée with semisweet chocolate, cocoa, and milk. It is firm like Jello, but has the texture of the most luxurious chocolate pudding inside.

I pour it into a square nonstick pan and unmold it on a cake stand. Then I heap berries in the center, dollop whipped cream on top of the berries, and serve. It's refreshing and cool and utterly delicious on a hot summer night, making a lovely presentation as well.

SPECIAL EQUIPMENT 1 (8- TO 9-INCH) SQUARE NONSTICK PAN; ELECTRIC HAND MIXER

3 ½ cups whole milk

2 (4-ounce) packages semisweet chocolate bars, broken

¼ cup plus 2 tablespoons Hershey's Special Dark Cocoa

¼ cup plus 3 tablespoons granulated sugar

1 teaspoon pure vanilla extract

½ cup cold water

2 packets plus 1 ½ teaspoons powdered gelatin

Whipped Cream

1 ½ cup heavy whipping cream

3 tablespoons granulated sugar

¼ teaspoon pure vanilla extract

To serve

1 pint strawberries

1 pint raspberries

Heat the milk and chocolate in a saucepan, stirring frequently to encourage the chocolate to melt. Add the cocoa and sugar and whisk until the chocolate, cocoa, and sugar are melted into the milk. Add vanilla and whisk.

Pour the water into a shallow bowl, sprinkle gelatin over the top, and stir once to combine. Let stand for 2 minutes, until the gelatin absorbs all the water.

Heat the milk mixture back to a point where little bubbles are forming around the edges, until it is almost, but not quite, boiling. Vigorously whisk the gelatin into the hot milk mixture and continue cooking and whisking for about 1 minute, or until the gelatin is dissolved.

Wet the inside of the nonstick pan, place it in a larger pan to catch any spills, and pour the chocolate mixture in all the way to the top of the nonstick pan. Cool to room temperature, cover with plastic wrap, and refrigerate for 6 hours or overnight.

Before unmolding, touch the jellied chocolate. If it is still tacky to the touch, it is not set yet. The top must be dry. To unmold, briefly submerge the pan in warm (not hot) water up to the rim for 10 seconds. Then dip a small sharp knife in warm water and carefully insert the tip of it around the top edges to dislodge the jelly. Place a chilled serving plate or cake stand over the top and invert. Gently shake and tap the top of the pan to unmold. Place the plate of jelly in the refrigerator until ready to serve.

WHIPPED CREAM

Pour the cream into a bowl and beat until soft peaks form. Sprinkle with sugar and vanilla and beat until soft peaks form again.

To serve the jelly, pile the berries in the center, top with soft mounds of whipped cream, and bring to the table to slice and serve.

BABA AU RHUM

Le Baba au Rhum LONGER | SERVES 8 TO 10

Invented in France, babas au rhum *are small bread-like cakes that are soaked in rum syrup. I make a large one in a decorative cake pan using pretty much the same recipe you would for a baba au rhum, savarin, brioche, or gugelhopf, all of which have similar dough. Sweet yeast breads take time to rise, so begin this one early in the day.*

SPECIAL EQUIPMENT CITRUS MICROPLANE; FOOD PROCESSOR; CANDY THERMOMETER; 1 (5- TO 6-CUP) DECORATIVE CAKE MOLD OR BUNDT PAN; PARCHMENT PAPER; ELECTRIC HAND MIXER

Baba

1 organic orange

4 large eggs, room temperature

2 teaspoons pure vanilla extract

1 teaspoon almond extract

2 cups all-purpose flour

2 cups cake flour

½ teaspoon salt

7 tablespoons granulated sugar, divided

½ cup milk

½ cup water

2 packages active dry yeast

5 tablespoons unsalted butter, melted, divided

Syrup

¾ cup water

1 cup granulated sugar

¼ cup organic orange juice

1 teaspoon pure vanilla extract

3 tablespoons dark rum

Glaze

½ cup orange marmalade

1 tablespoon light corn syrup

1 tablespoon rum

Whipped Cream

2 cups heavy whipping cream, chilled

3 tablespoons superfine sugar

2 teaspoons pure vanilla extract

2 tablespoons nonfat or skim powdered milk

To Serve

Assorted fresh berries or fruit of choice

Confectioner's sugar

BABA

Zest the orange using the microplane then juice it. Divide the zest in half. Reserve the juice for the syrup.

With a fork, beat the eggs with the vanilla and almond extracts.

Sift both flours into the bowl of a food processor. Add the salt and 6 tablespoons sugar; pulse for 5 seconds to combine.

Pour the milk and water into a saucepan and warm over low heat to 100 degrees F on the candy thermometer. Pour into a shallow bowl, whisk in

continued >

remaining sugar, sprinkle the yeast over the top, whisk, then allow to stand for at least 5 minutes to become foamy and bloom.

Add the foamy yeast, the egg mixture, half of the orange zest, and 3 tablespoons butter to the flour in the food processor; process until a smooth dough forms.

Turn out the dough into a lightly oiled bowl. It will be very sticky and soft. Cover with plastic wrap then with a thick kitchen towel and let rise for 1 hour, until it has doubled in volume.

Brush the remaining butter over the inside of the baking pan, taking care to cover any inside crevices.

Punch down the dough and use a metal spoon or rubber spatula to transfer it into the mold. Cover with plastic wrap, then a towel, and leave to rise for 20 minutes while you preheat the oven to 350 degrees F.

Bake for 20–25 minutes, until golden brown on top. Remove from oven, cool in the pan for 2 minutes, then unmold onto a wire rack set over a plate or parchment paper.

SYRUP

Bring the water, sugar, and orange juice to a boil. Remove from the heat and whisk in the vanilla and rum. Poke holes all over the top of the cake with a skewer and pour the boiling syrup over the top of the cake to soak in. Do this several times, using up any accumulated syrup from the bottom of the plate, until the cake is drenched and thoroughly soaked.

Wrap the cake in plastic wrap to keep the moisture in and let set for 20 minutes.

GLAZE

Melt the marmalade with the corn syrup and rum and brush the resulting glaze all over the cake. Allow to set for 15 minutes.

WHIPPED CREAM

Pour the cream into a bowl and beat with the mixer until soft peaks form. Sprinkle with sugar, vanilla, and powdered milk and beat until soft peaks form again.

TO SERVE

Serve slices of cake with berries or fruit and confectioner's sugar sprinkled over the top.

TIP

You can omit the rum throughout the recipe and substitute orange juice.

ACKNOWLEDGMENTS

My special thanks to Steven Rothfeld, world-class photographer and friend, for agreeing to fly into a snowy blizzard to work with me on this, our fourth cookbook together. Your vision in turning my creations into pure art inspires me every day to do better.

Thanks to my agent, Deborah Ritchken, for her unflagging encouragement and for getting our projects in motion. You are amazing.

My thanks to Barbara Barrielle, movie producer, writer, and food stylist for her imaginative and artistic food styling. You are invaluable and a great friend.

Thanks to Carrie Pfeifer, my right hand during the photo shoot, for her good humor, for keeping me on time, for giving me a shoulder to lean on, and for anticipating all my needs. And thanks, as always, to dear Hélène Lautier, cookbook author and friend, for all French translations.

As always, my sincere thanks go to the entire team at Gibbs Smith for their extreme professionalism, enthusiasm, and for designing such beautiful books. Special thanks to my editor, Michelle Branson, for her support, patience, suggestions, and focused intention to create absolute perfection.

To my recipe testers: Barbara Michelson, Beth Marinello, Sarah Hodge, Sandy Sidwell, Christine Dutton, Leah Klein, Debbie Royer, Jann Mumford, Neal Oldford, Cathy Erway, Kristy Stephens Ammann, and Karen Schwartz Wirima—a huge thank you for your hard work, for testing and retesting, and for always offering to do more.

I want to say special thanks to my friends who are always there to support and encourage me: the Fairfield Road taste testers, Sandy Taylor, Susan Laughlin, Kathleen Kennedy, Laura Elise Brown, Betsy Callas, Jen Cartmell, Jane Cartmell, the Mann family, George Sheinberg, Heather Pilley, Prudence Sam May Plusch, Judith Zouck, Hélène Lautier, Blandine Beaulieu, Grove Hafela, Jenny Hartin, Foster Thalheimer, Margaux Eckert, Debbie Thomas, Barbara Michelson, and Steve Davis.

I would also like to express my gratitude to Le Creuset, Revol, and Emile Henry for kindly providing us with such beautiful products from France to shoot our dessert recipes on.

And my heartfelt thanks go to James Barclay, who tasted and judged most of the desserts in this book, for his encouragement, and for so graciously offering his home to our crew to shoot the beautiful photographs. His kitchen floor had flour footprints, and every doorknob was covered in chocolate during the process. With all my love, I dedicate this book to you.

PLANTES D'INFUSION
ISSUES de l'AGRICULTURE
BIOLOGIQUE
ou de cueillettes sauvages
€
2,80€ le paquet

INDEX